Front

Dedicated to my teacher, Fook Yueng

Copyright: Steve Gray. Full name: Steven Jeffrey Gray

First published 3/1/2019 by Kindle ebooks as A Lineage of Dragons.

Editor - Nick Vasey: nickvasey.com/writing-editing
Website - alineageofdragons.com

THE MAGUS OF SEATTLE

Contents

INTRODUCTION

This book is mostly about my own personal experiences, but includes things I have been told by the people in the book and by my kung fu and chi kung brothers. Some of these brothers have been close enough to the people in this book to be considered authorities. Of course, second hand information can have mistakes, and where I have heard conflicting stories I have pointed them out accordingly. This book also contains the results of a couple of decades of random and casual reading knowledge, which, in some cases, I have dovetailed into my own experiences. I did my reading for my own entertainment and education, not for writing a book, so I have no footnotes or sources or anything of that sort to offer, unless noted. Some of these stories may be difficult to believe. I myself would not have been able to believe some of them thirty years ago. So please, be my guest and believe or not believe, whatever you wish, as you wish.

The internet website - alineageofdragons.com is for sharing more of the background and cultivation methods described, and for sharing some additional stories which are not included in the book.

Steve Gray

I hope this book helps you along your way in some way.

Steve Gray

1 - THE ANDES MOUNTAINS

When civilization started in China around four thousand years ago the ancient sages moved up into the mountains to, as they put it, "get far above the dust of civilization," and their practices came to be known as chi kung.

I feel so lucky to have moved here into this mountain wilderness. The stars are brilliant tonight. At this altitude, so far from population centers there's no light pollution, it is so dark when there's no moon, the stars shine in a way you will never see in low lying or civilized areas of the world. The Milky Way is stretched across the sky like a bright band of fog, and Mars has just risen over the crest of the Andes mountain range, the continental divide, which you can drive to from here in around an hour. Even on the blackest cloudless nights you can see that the mountains are truly black whereas the sky is considerably brighter. That's because the sky glows. In two ways. On a clear night it comes from the glow of billions of stars and galaxies that fill the whole sky, and yet are so distant that they coalesce into a faint fog of light. A light which is bright enough to show you your way even on a moonless night. During the day the sky glows like a soft blue neon light because the air in the atmosphere scatters light of that color from our sun.

Sometimes at night, during the rainy season, the sky to the east shines with constant flashes of light. That's due to frequent thunderstorms in the nearby Amazon, and the reason there is no sound of thunder is because the mountain chain blocks it. Silent thunder. During those thunderstorms it can be dry here, even though those storms are only a few miles to the east. When it rains real hard here, the sound is so loud on metal roofs that you have to yell in a person's ear in order to talk, and I have to wear ear plugs to keep my ears from hurting. It usually rains hard like that for only ten or fifteen minutes; if it goes on for a half hour or more it gets a little scary, and we start to wonder how much of the road or the mountain might be gone the next morning.

Where I am here in Southern Ecuador is a low point in the Andes mountain chain because the Amazon river used to run to the Pacific through this area, and cut its way down through the mountains for millions of years until the new mountains began rising too quickly, finally blocking it's way and forcing the Amazon to run to the Atlantic. The locals say, "donde los Andes se agachan," which means, where the Andes crouch down. Due to this we can see the nearby continental divide, which is at around 10,000 ft altitude, from our location of 7000 ft altitude. The local highest peak, Cerro Toledo, which you can see from here and also drive to the top of, is at 12,000 ft altitude. It's one of the only roads in South America that goes nowhere, to no population center. It was built in order to put a radar installation on the mountain top for the longest running territorial dispute, ending in armed invasion, in the Western hemisphere. Ecuador and Peru were fighting over a big chunk of the Amazon which is but a stone's throw down the East side of the continental ridge here.

This area is known as a cloud forest. We are also next door to the Podocarpus National Park that runs along the top of the Andes in this area. The Podocarus has more biodiversity than any other place on Earth. When I discovered that this land I bought has morning mist clouds drifting through the peaks and valleys, reminiscent of the ancient Chinese landscape paintings, I loved it even more. Sometimes those old Taoist cloud mountain paintings depicted a dragon or two peeking out from the mist.

It doesn't get too cold here. The locals call it the land of eternal springtime and the temperature is pretty much always between 60 and 80 degrees F (16 to 27 deg. C.). The popular nearby tourist town of Vilcabamba is located in what is called the Sacred Valley, because the Inca Emperor used to go there to vacation, and due to the longevity of the locals it is also one of the five official "Shangri Las" of the world. Fortunately, here in the Land of Eternal Springtime at our altitude there are few bugs and mosquitos, no screens are needed on doors or windows.

Our water comes out of ridge top springs and is so pure that it's almost like distilled water. Our air comes to us after being purified and energized by passing over the billions of trees and through the countless thunderstorms in the high Amazon. The air has a sparkle and an energy that is so rare. The blue sky is so blue, such a deep strong blue that makes you love to look at the sky. You may notice, if you look straight overhead into the super blue sky, that there is a darker area there and the sky is brighter around the horizon. That is because due to the altitude and the clean air we are able to see a little bit of deep space.

And there are the dragons. It turns out that there are dragons in these mountains, several visitors have commented on being able to sense them, and one channeler who visited said that the dragons are happy that I'm here, and are providing protection for us and the little valley and its surrounding ridges that I bought with my life savings from the US. I don't know if the dragons were already here and called me or if they congregated after I came. I know of one lady who saw and heard from a dragon in a nearby valley.

This land of dragons, which is newly named Tien Shan after the great mountain chain in Asia from which comes my Chi Kung, gives us broad views of endless mountain chains from our little mountain top.

Here's a little example of what life on the farm here is like. I just went into the house and Spirit was standing in the middle of the kitchen. Spirit is our little black horse, he has a short nose that makes him look like a colt and he's as cute as a button. I left the door from the kitchen to the veranda open, as we frequently do. Spirit had eaten most of the fruits and vegetables, knocked things off the counters, and slobbered all over the floor, making a huge mess. It seems that the local who told me horses don't walk on tile because they will slip and fall had some incomplete knowledge. Maybe a big horse would slip and fall but since Spirit is small and lightweight he was able to manage his escape. His feet were slipping around, but he didn't fall.

When Spirit had only been here a day or two I went down to give the horses some bananas. I gave a banana to Spirit and then turned around to give one to another horse. When I turned my back on him he bit my butt, so I turned back around and slapped him in the face.

We let a couple of the horses roam freely around the house area, inside the main fence. They help keep the grass trimmed and leave us a lot of top quality fertilizer just a stone's throw from the front door.

2 - THE ART OF FLYING

When I was still very young I started to love birds and I loved the idea of flying. I was a child prodigy of sorts when it came to drawing and painting, and birds were my favorite subject to draw.

When I was around ten years old and living in Caracas, Venezuela, I began to have an interesting series of dreams. I dreamed I was on top of a hill, looking down a green grassy slope. In front of me was a smooth area going down like a sloping runway or street. There were three short level areas crossing this. It was like some of the steep streets in San Francisco, which level off at each intersection where there is a cross street. There was a big flat field at the bottom of this slope.

I didn't see my body, so I didn't see any wings, but in the dream I knew I had wings. I went running down the hill flapping my wings as hard as I could until I got to the big field at the bottom.

The next night I had a similar dream. I went running down the hill flapping my wings, and this time at the end of each of the level areas I was able to make a little jump into the air, like from a ski jump, and clearing a little distance until touching onto the slope, continuing running. The third night the hops into the air from the level spots were bigger and I was able to make it further down the slopes before touching down.

The fourth night, after running down the slope once again I was able to take off from the first little level part, and flapping my wings hard I was able to stay in the air, skimming above the slope although still going downwards, until I gained enough speed to fly free of ground air cushion and was able to circle once around the grassy field at the bottom.

Then the dreams stopped. I didn't know it till more than sixty years later, but this was my first link I know of, this series of dreams was my initiation into the realm of dragons, something which will be explained in detail later.

One thing that has stood out to me over time is how the dreams of flying and levitation are a lot of fun, and while other dreams are quickly forgotten I have remembered the dreams of flying rather well.

After that, as a young man, I had dreams of many different kinds of flying.

The earlier flying dreams were ones where I would begin hopping or jumping along some sidewalk as if I was bouncing on a big pogo stick. Then the jumps would start getting bigger. I would jump six feet, then ten, then fifteen, arcing higher up in the air each time for a bigger view of the neighborhood. When crossing a big avenue I had to jump all the way across to the other sidewalk, over the vehicles, so I had to land just on the edge and then push off extra hard, flying over the heads of pedestrians, who never saw me.

At other times I had dreams of doing a kind of acrobatic type of jumping. These consisted of me running along and jumping up to grab a tree branch, swinging around it and flinging myself off into the air to grab another tree branch, swing around that, and fling myself off in a new direction. It was like a gymnast performing on bars, like monkeys flying through trees, or like the intense acrobatics required of the Monkey King in the Chinese Opera. I mention this because my chi kung teacher, Mr. Yueng, played the part of the Monkey King, who was the star of the opera, and because I feel I have a past life link to similar ways of moving.

It is said that sometimes these shamanic kinds of experiences result from being touched by a shaman. I spent my entire boyhood growing up in Latin America and the Philippine Islands, and may have been touched by some shaman without knowing it.

Or maybe it was the Shaman who touched me when I hired him to take me and my wife snorkeling on his boat out on the Belize barrier reef. He grabbed me by the arm a few times when I was climbing into the boat. They said he was a powerful curandero, a healer with plant and spirit medicine, a good shaman. He was proud of the glass bottom boat he had made, and told me how the two parts of the V bottom were pieces of one inch thick bulletproof glass that he had imported from New York. With that glass bottom it was not a problem to occasionally bump against, or scrape along, a bit of the corral reef.

The dreams of flying and levitation really got intense a couple of years after I became a student of Mr. Yueng. Some of it came from the chi energy he used to give me each week in class, plus probably some kind of psychic link. I learned later that he was so psychic that he was commonly connected to me mentally. Also, people tend to dream about things which they are learning.

These dreams I had were mostly when I was in my forties, during the time I was Mr. Yueng's apprentice.

There were two types, one was flying like a bird flapping its wings and the other was flying like levitation.

In the beginning the dreams were of flying like a bird. It wasn't easy, I knew I had to build up my chest and arm strength so in the beginning I spent plenty of time standing on the ground and flapping my arms/wings, focussing more on the push down. Early on, I was able to fly some short hops off level ground, so in a way these were a continuation of my first series of flying dreams when I was around ten in Venezuela, where I took off running down the grassy slope. Later I was able to make longer flights, yet I was still very aware of all the work being I had to do with my chest muscles and of their limited endurance. Sometimes my flights were in nature and at other times I circled places like seaside citadels. Later the flights became easier and there was no sense of muscles getting tired but rather limited endurance. Sometimes I had to take off running down streets crowded by buildings, wires, and bridges and avoid all those obstacles while taking off.

Other dreams involved rising up or floating up, some with the aid of flapping wings but most were without. A number of these vertical ascents involved rising up through a tangle of branches or telephone lines that were overhead. In the beginning these would stop me but later I had better luck at drifting through the tangle, and continued upwards into clear space. Often I would rise up above my neighborhood and see my house and the neighbors' houses while flying around the neighborhood a bit, and then gliding back down.

I used to play one game which was fun, I would crouch down and jump up as high as possible while throwing my arms up high to reach up and grab a big armful of air and then push down. Basically like pushing off hard from the side of a swimming pool and doing a giant breast stroke, then seeing how far I got. This is something I used to practice when I was a kid in the swimming pools we had in some of our houses in South America; only in this case it was going up vertically like a bird does when it leaps up and grabs that first big wing full of air in order to take off.

The other dreams were of the levitation type, where you glide through the air just by using will power, or intent ... or something ... having a lot of energy helps. Sometimes I would jump up to the ceiling of high rooms, like auditoriums for example, then jump around, bouncing off the walls, pushing off with my legs till I got to the other side or the ceiling, and then pushing off again in a different direction. I used to practice similar things in real life. I played at underwater acrobatics and aerobatics in the deep end of swimming pools.

The levitating type of dreams included sailing down corridors in big buildings, gliding silently and unseen above the heads of the people there. At other times I found myself drifting softly through deep basement tunnels where there was no one.

The most wonderful one, by far, was when I found myself on a naked rocky planet with a dark and starry sky. I was in an exotic land formation shaped like a gigantic rocky valley with a flat floor

for a bottom, like it was a dried lake or a gigantic impact crater on the moon, with mountains
around the edges. Across the middle of this valley, dividing it in two, was a narrow bridge of land,
like an elevated rock pathway. I sat on the ground,
and using intent I zoomed across the land bridge
to the other side and back at extremely high
speed, and then back to the starting point. It was
several miles to the other side and I went across
in a couple of seconds. The very high speed was
exhilarating. I know now that this kind of dream
practice came from past life experiences and from
dream lessons from my Chi Kung teacher, Mr.
Yueng. It also is some more practicing for the future. I feel that some of the places I saw were
due to astral projection and that my spirit was
there, perhaps inhabiting a bird as is a common
shamanic theme both in Asia and the Americas,
where the shaman can go into the body of an animal and see what it sees.

When I was sixteen I completed my last two years
of high school in the US, where I lived at the Culver Military Academy boarding school in Culver
Indiana. Famous among American high schools as
being at the top of the list when it came to quality
education, and that as back when America itself
was known for quality education. My parents sent
me there because the three American high schools
in Caracas Venezuela were of such poor quality
that they were not recognized by American uni-

versities, and also because my parents thought I was a discipline problem. They thought I needed to learn some good old military style discipline! The main motivation though was my poor grades. I was getting Ds and Fs on my report cards, so my parents were called in to have a conference with the school principal. In the meeting, my dad told the principal I had tested earlier as having an IQ of 145 and so the reason for my poor grades was obviously because the school and teachers stank. In Culver Military academy I got mostly As and graduated near the top of my class. This was because I liked the challenge. I didn't really mind the military part, living in barracks and marching in parades with a heavy rifle on my shoulder was just a slight burden. The good thing is that it gave us all a taste of the military, and 99% of the students there swore they would never go into the military, an excellent decision considering the war in Vietnam had just swung into full steam.

I had planned on going to the Air Force University to learn aeronautical engineering and become a fighter pilot, then later retire from the Air Force and get a job as an airline pilot. However, during my last year in high school I became slightly near-sighted, which disqualified me from being a pilot, so I didn't go into the Air Force. This left me completely aimless. I didn't feel like going to a university but I had to because that was the way to get out of the Vietnam draft. My dad suggested I go to the University of Washington because it had an excellent school of aeronautical engineering and it had links to and was in the same city as the Boeing Aircraft company, where I could then get a job.

Maybe it was pre-destiny that caused me to go to the same university where Bruce Lee started nine years earlier, because we ended up having the same main teacher who lived in Seattle.

By the way, the reason for all this talk of flying is because flying is one thing that dragons revel in.

.

3 - THE BRUCE LEE CONNECTION

Master Fook Yueng

It is common knowledge that Ip Man was Bruce Lee's teacher. He was a good one too, very influential in Bruce's development. Many people naturally assume Ip Man was Bruce's main teacher, but Ip Man was more like Bruce's high school teacher and a secretive man in Seattle, who was Bruce's uncle, was his university and master level teacher. In fact Bruce came to Seattle to live with him while going to the University of Washington.

Mr. Yueng asked me to not write about him until after he passed away, for reasons that will be explained shortly. Fook Yueng was born in 1915 in the Cantonese province of Fujian in the Southeast corner of China, and he passed away in Seattle, Washington on April of 2012 at the age of 97, from a stroke.

Mr. Yueng joined the Chinese opera when very young, at around the age of ten. Normally this happened because the family couldn't afford to feed them, and sold them to the Opera. The training the boys in those operas endured was brutal;

it was much more difficult than anything similar that exists today. The martial artists had to get up at four in the morning and work out hard for two hours before even being allowed to use the restroom. The opera was divided into two classes of people. The singers and the martial artists, with the singers going about with a snooty attitude towards the martial artists, who were considered low class.

The opera martial artists kept a low profile because their opera training included a secret version of Wing Chun, which was banned by the Chinese government. Additionally, believe it or not, their traveling opera was a cover for a troupe of anti government assassins!

Mr. Yueng was one of the martial artists, and he was so good that he became the Monkey King, the star of the opera. The Monkey King performance consisted of the hero, the Monkey King, running, jumping, and somersaulting through a group of three or four others, all of whom swinging staffs, spears and swords at him at the same time. While doing this he was taking their weapons away from them and then throwing them back. So the Monkey King and the weapons would be flying through the air all over the place. That performance is without a doubt the most advanced acrobatic performances ever seen. Bruce Lee's dad, Lee Hoi-Chuen, also joined the opera as a boy, and like Mr. Yueng he also played the part of the Monkey King, making Mr. Yueng and Lee Hoi-Chuen the clos-est of kung fu brothers. Kung fu brotherhood was taken very seriously, because the opera was their family, and thus Mr. Yueng was Bruce Lee's uncle.

The opera company was called the Red Boat Opera Company, RBOC, and it consisted of some Chinese junks (small ships), that were painted red. They traveled up and down the coast of China and along its rivers, giving opera performances in different cities. When they arrived at a new city they were required to have a challenge fight between the hero of the boat and the hero of the city. If the city won the opera had to pay taxes to the city. If the the boat won then they didn't have to pay taxes. These were serious no-holds-barred fights and some of the fighters were crippled or killed during these fights. Mr. Yueng told me about a kick boxer on the boat whose legs were so strong he could put the anchor over the side with his leg. This fellow had his Achilles tendon ripped out by an Eagle claw fighter, which probably made his career difficult for a while. Mr. Yueng was some-times the boat's hero. One time he told me that no one was ever able to hit him, which implies that he never lost a fight.

Once, their ship went to San Francisco for a few months to put on an opera performance, and that is when Bruce was born, automatically making him a US citizen. It was at this time Mr. Yueng de-cided to stay in the US because the Japanese had invaded China and he didn't want to get involved in a war. So he jumped ship, and after a short time in California moved to Seattle, Washington, where he lived for the rest of his life.

One little known fact about the the RBOC is that they were opponents of the Qing Dynasty and used their opera as cover while engaging in espionage and assassination of government officials. Their identities as Chinese opera performers provided perfect cover for their martial arts and assassination training.

The RBOC is also credited with the development of Red Boat Wing Chun, which is said to be the originator of all Wing Chun. Its inner methods remain hidden. It was a softer and more internal style of Wing Chun than you see these days and was outlawed by the Chinese government because it was so effective.

The flashy moves of opera style martial arts were not used in assassinations, which required specialized skills. Even though assassinations were generally done with poison or knives, their targets were usually protected by bodyguards who, when they discovered an intruder, would seize the person, yell for help, and then subdue and hold them for questioning. Therefore Wing Chun was developed to silence the opponent immediately. This explains some of the aspects underpinning Wing Chun, such as its focus on close-range combat and its frequent use of strikes to the throat and diaphragm.

It stands to reason that since Mr. Yueng was one of stars of the RBOC, and was sometimes champion of the boat during matches in different cities, that he was also one of the assassins. His character matches the profile of a trained assassin as well, embodying the traits of being calm, well grounded, sincere, clever, and loving life in a joyous manner. An honorable assassin, someone who has a perspective on life which makes him appreciate living so much more, than if he had some other kind of job.

Once I asked Mr. Yueng who his kung fu teacher was and he said that everyone in China was his teacher. He explained that because he had been a good looking kid and talented that a lot of masters liked him and offered to teach him. In this way he was exposed to many different systems of training as the opera company traveled around China. In all he learned around one hundred different martial arts, and he knew them so well, they eventually blended together into what became his own personal system. He liked Tai Chi a lot too, so the main arts he used in his personal blend were Tai Chi and Wing Chun but included strong elements of Bagua and Praying Mantis. He told me: "take the best from each system and leave the rest," which is also something which Bruce wrote. I don't really know much about Bruce, this story is really about his teacher.

When Bruce moved to the US he arrived at San Francisco where Mr. Yueng went to pick him up at the boat pier. The first thing Bruce did when he met Mr. Yueng is put his hands out and say "Chi Sao" which is a type of Wing Chun sensitivity game like pushing hands or sticky hands in Tai Chi. Although Bruce was very good, he was not able to get any advantage over Mr. Yueng, but Mr. Yueng could tap him at will. Mr. Yueng took Bruce up to Seattle and got him a job at Ruby Chow's restaurant, which was a luxuriously appointed fine dining establishment in the Southeast part of downtown Seattle. Mr. Yueng was a cook there and was living in an apartment on the top floor of the big three story building. Bruce moved in with him and lived there while working as a waiter and going to the University of Washington. Bruce lived there for three years before moving out, but continued to learn from Mr. Yueng for a total of eight years. Mr. Yueng encouraged Bruce to visit other teachers in the area while he was still with him, in order to get a broader perspective of the martial arts.

Mr. Yueng told me that Bruce practiced very hard, often getting up very early in the morning and working out for three hours before heading off to school.

Mr. Yueng didn't want people to know he taught

Bruce because, he only taught him as a friend and uncle, and didn't want people challenging him to fights or bothering him for lessons. Bruce liked it too because then he got to say he made it all up. The main reason Mr. Yueng didn't want me to write about him and Bruce till after he passed away, was because Mr. Yueng's closest kung fu brother, Bruce's dad, was friends with the Ip Man family and Mr. Yueng didn't want to cause Ip Man to lose face.

Mr. Yueng taught Bruce a Kung Fu form called Jeet Kun, and what Bruce went on to teach didn't really have a lot to do with that form but he liked the name so he added Do to it to appeal to the Karate people. Bruce didn't know there was another higher level, named Shen Kun, which is basically the Jedi stuff, which Mr. Yueng taught to a few people some decades later.

At that time Americans had discovered Karate and it was becoming popular, but Kung Fu was unheard of. Mr. Yueng and Bruce were shocked by the crudeness and stupidity of American Karate, which was actually a bastardization of real Japanese Karate, so they decided to show the Western world how cool Kung Fu was. You see, after being defeated by the Americans and being subjected to the rule of the Western barbarians, the Japanese were in no way going to share the high level Karate stuff with their shockingly crude and rude dominators. They taught them some forms, katas, but none of the nasty details of how those forms could be used. What they taught the Americans, for example, were methods of fighting for those wearing heavy armor to people who wouldn't be wearing armor. Now some Japanese masters are sharing some effective Karate stuff with their foreigners. Even real Ninjitsu has surfaced. personally I prefer Ninjitsu, which is softer and sneakier. The Ninjas are descendants of Chinese chi kung masters who migrated to Japan long ago; they had a war with the Samurai and lost, but went into hiding rather than killing themselves as was the traditional Japanese way.

Since Mr. Yueng and Bruce came from an opera background it was natural they decided to use cinema, the new opera, in order for Bruce to demonstrate the kung fu and acrobatics he knew, and it worked remarkably well. The rest is history - except for the secret part about Bruce's main Kung Fu teacher, a most powerful Chi Kung master who kept to the shadows - which is what this book is about.

I haven't read any of Bruce's books but I've seen popular quotes from him on the internet, and most of them sounded familiar because they are similar to things that Mr. Yueng told me. Therefore it seems Bruce learned those same quotes from Mr. Yueng.

There is already a great deal written about Bruce,

so there isn't much more to say about him except for one thing which is not so well known, and that is that Bruce taught more to his first student, Jesse Glover, than to others who are using the JKD brand name. Bruce became friends with Jesse, who was a Judo champion, while he was still with Mr. Yueng. He used Jesse as a practice partner to test and perfect the methods he was learning so Jesse had the great opportunity to be there when all the theory and basics were being worked out. Once Jesse heard Bruce say that if he taught, to not call it Jeet Kun Do, because it's such an adaptable and personal art. For example. the source of it, which is now named Fook Yueng Chuan, with its ten thousand techniques, is just that, super adaptable. Bruce explained that since everyone is different, different methods work better for different people, and Jeet Kun Do was his own personal art. Later though it appears that Bruce did sell his "Franchise" to some of his other students.

It seems to me that when Bruce was teaching his later students he focussed more on technique and left out the basics that held the keys to his kind of mastery. This is a common tradition among teachers in the Chinese internal arts, to not share enough to allow the student to possibly become better than the teacher, holding back for self preservation reasons, so they can retain their position as head of the school. With Jesse it was different though. Jesse was Bruce's fellow explorer of the "Way of the Intercepting Fist." He obeyed Bruce's sentiment about not calling it Jeet Kun Do and instead called his art Non Classical Kung Fu, NCKF.

Therefore I feel that for the aspiring self defense student who wants to follow as closely as possible the master Bruce Lee, that they can get closer to the original by checking out NCKF rather than JKD. There is no doubt that JKD is a most effective and deadly self defense art. It's simply that NCKF is closer to the original source. The further you get from the original grandmaster, the more likely it is to get to a more fundamentalist aspect of things. In this case fundamentalist aspect refers to using hard style whereas the source of it all is rather soft, doesn't require much effort, and has an outstanding economy of movement.

Mr. Yueng left the RBOC after around a decade and worked for an herbal medicine doctor in Southern China for a while. He told me that sometimes they would go hiking and camping in the wilderness for over a week at a time while looking for wild medicinal herbs. He was the young assistant who got to carry most of the plants they picked, and he learned things like how to defend yourself if attacked by a tiger, which he taught to me. He said that people would pay for their medical advice and herbs with food, so sometimes they would eat well, sometimes they didn't get much to eat, and other times when there were no customers, they went hungry. Mr. Yueng returned to the opera and stayed with them till he got to San Fransisco. After moving to Seattle he got a job as a cook working at Ruby Chow's luxury Chinese Restaurant. Later he opened his own restaurant in Everett, Washington, which he named the Golden Dragon.

Running a restaurant is a lot of work, and Mr. Yueng told me he used to work around twenty hours a day at it. He would get up before sunrise and go to the Seattle public market to buy fresh food and veggies when it opened bright and early. Then he'd go up to Everett and start preparing the food. He'd stay at the restaurant all day and night, thenhave to clean up after the midnight closing, then drive back home to Seattle for a couple of hours of sleep.

Sometimes Andy, my first Tai Chi teacher, would go up there before closing with some other guys and they would play around with self defense methods after the restaurant closed.

The Golden Dragon had a bar, and sometimes the customers would get a little drunk and rowdy and start yelling. Mr. Yueng would go over to them and calmly grab the guy with one hand on a pressure point on the person's wrist and his other hand on a pressure point on their elbow. He would press on these points enough to cause just enough pain to get the customer to follow him peacefully out the door. None of the customers knew what he was doing; it looked like he was helping a little old lady to cross the street. Once outside he'd let them go and say: "OK, you go home now," and sometimes they would swing at him, with results that you might imagine. With your typical sauced amateur it takes them more than a second to even wind up for their first punch, and Mr. Yueng was trained to end a fight in one second, so he was way ahead of the game. Of course he didn't hurt them much, just showed them the folly of their ways.

The long hours of work at the restaurant plus the lack of sleep took their toll, and Mr. Yueng got sick. One brother told me he had a heart attack and heart problems, and another told me he got cancer, so I don't know which it was, but he sold his restaurant, quit working, and started to focus on chi kung. Illness can provide just the right motivation to do chi kung a lot, and so it was that Mr. Yueng really got into it, with outstanding results.

He retired from restauranting at around age 70 and I started with him when he was about 76. His Chi Kung healed him of his illness, and went on to give him super health and a lot of chi power in only six years. Of course he was already well primed for it because he had been exposed to a culture of Chi Kung in his martial arts training in the opera, which housed a secret sect of chi power cultivators.

Sometimes people ask me how Bruce really died. Since I was in this little family that Bruce was a part of the subject came up a couple of times. When I asked Mr. Yueng about it he said "too much sex," but I think he said it that way moreso for my benefit, because I've always had these sex maniac tendencies. Another brother told me the same thing in a little more detail: Bruce was killed by a lover with a poison needle or a poisoned sharpened fingernail.

The reason for this possibility is rather obvious when you think about it. The Chinese take their martial arts *very* seriously. The different schools normally accepted each other and there was some conflict between them, but not a lot. Then this kid comes from America and tells them all that his art is better than theirs, and that he made it up himself. That was bad enough, but then he proved it by beating all challengers. In this way he made a lot of powerful enemies in China, which explains why he would have been assassinated by one of his many lovers.

Speaking of sharpened poisoned fingernails, on both hands Mr. Yueng had elongated fingernails on his little fingers. These were cut so that they had a slight point to them, like a ninety degree angle at the tip, and they also had sharpened edges. I tried growing my little fingernails longer in the same manner but the only thing that came of it was that

I would cut myself when I picked my nose. I asked Andy, my Tai Chi teacher, who was his adopted son, what the long fingernails were for, and he said that you could cut the forehead of someone you were fighting and the blood would get in their eyes and prevent them from seeing. However this would not end a fight in one second, so I doubted it. I then asked Mr. Yueng what the longer fingernails were for and by way of explanation he put his palm on my face and then casually brushed the little fingernail sideways a millimeter in front of my eye. Cutting someone's eyeball will usually end a fight in one second, and it gives them something to think about next time they want to attack someone, because they may not want to lose their last eye. Blinding attackers is one frequently used technique in our system. It ends a fight instantly, with the following benefits, the aggressor can't chase you when you run away, they will never be able to mug or attack someone again, and they can't identify you in a police lineup. Those things are not of any concern on the sporting side of martial arts training, and that's the side you usually get at the local neighborhood strip mall dojo.

4 - "WE ARE DRAGONS"

Let me tell you in no uncertain terms that I was certain dragons did not exist. I was like a Mr. Science, I loved science and physics, and along with that came the standard baggage consisting of a thin egoistic belief that there was no spirit world. I was a mechanically minded real world kind of guy and I never suspected that my visitor could be a dragon ... but I'm getting ahead of the story. Not only was I certain that dragons did not exist, I was sure that if there were any kind spirit beings that they would never have anything to do with me.

Well I was wrong again.

After I had been going to practice at Mr. Yueng's house each week for around a year, he told me I would start to see faces while I was meditating and to just ignore them. It started happening right after he told me, while I was sitting meditating in bed, before going to sleep. It certainly is mysterious what was happening, and it happened a lot. While I was sitting meditating with my eyes closed, a face would appear in front of me about three feet away, looking at me, looking in my eyes. The face would stay there for maybe three or four seconds and then evaporate. I didn't recognize any of them, I had no idea who they were, or why they showed up. It didn't arouse my interest, nor was I curious, so I just ignored them like my teacher told me to. Almost all, but not all, of the faces I saw were human. I mentioned this once to a meditator who advised that seeing these faces was me working through my karma from what must have included plenty of past lives, considering how many faces there were.

Seeing faces was not convincing evidence to me that I was connecting with spirit beings in any way, but around that time something happened that was mind blowingly convincing.

It was back in the days of the early internet, and AOL had just invented public internet social forums. I met a lady through the Buddhism AOL forums and I thought she was kind of cute, probably because she sent me a 'cute' picture and didn't tell me she had a boyfriend. After knowing her for around a year she wrote that her boyfriend was in the hospital because he had acid thrown in his face, and she wanted me to pray for his healing.

I had never prayed for anything before so it was a new thing for me to try out. I figured to heal something like a face ruined by acid wasn't your every day run of the mill kind of healing request and it would take a real miracle to fix. I had read about Babaji Nagaraj in the Book "Autobiography of a Yogi". Babaji Nagaraj was born around 1800 years ago, he became an energy being before age 18, and is able to manifest a physical body if he wishes. An avatar is a person who is an incarnation of god, and there is at least one avatar on the planet at all times. Babaji is a mahavatar that is capable of real miracles so I decided to appeal to him. Mahavatar means great avatar. As an aside here, I learned that the Siddha Yoga that Babaji used to become an ascended master is similar to my Tien Shan Chi Kung.

I didn't know the person's name, and I had read that when you pray for something that you should be demanding about it. So, out loud, I said: "Babaji, I want you to heal this guy, and I want you to do it now, so just DO it!"

but the answer came right back: "Do it yourSELF" with an extra accent on self. Never in my wildest dreams did I expect to get an answer back, so that was special!

It sounds just like someone talking in your ear. There was absolutely no question that this answer came from outside myself, not in the slightest like the little self talk internal voice that some people dialogue with. It resulted in a cascade of realizations that occurred over a period of some years. The first one was a big one. There actually *are* invisible people out there that can talk to you! There really is a spirit world, and you really can relate to it. The first realization I had about this particular scenario was that I figured he was telling me off for bothering him, so the first lesson was 'do not bother avatars with selfish requests'.

Later the lady told me that her boyfriend was a punk drug dealer that was trying to weasel in on the Mafia's territory, in Las Vegas of all places. Not real swift.

Clearly the boyfriend asked for what he got, he got his karma delivered to his face. He asked for it and I realized that Babaji knew all about it even though I didn't know the guy's name, and he would not interfere with the guy's karma. That may have been the reason that he sounded annoyed at my request.

I had other thoughts, like why did he tell me to do it? Was he saying that I could heal something like that, or was he saying that he couldn't heal something like that? I didn't think he was saying I could heal it because i'm not a healer kind of guy and don't do it ... maybe he was saying it could be possible. I had another thought, why did he bother to answer me when he probably gets a hundred similar requests every minute? So you see, I had only questions and no answers.

I continued to see faces of strangers appear to me while meditating, but once it was notably different, and disconcerting. This time three beings came to see me, and I saw their whole bodies. They were standing further away, like about fifteen feet away, off to the left, and I knew they were demons! How did I know they were demons? I don't know, but it spooked me so much I stopped meditating. To give you an idea of what demons look like, picture the bad guys, the arms dealer aliens, in the movie "The Fifth Element," although not so cartoonish like in the movie, with a much more serious look, and seriously threatening aura.

Then the next night the three demons appeared again. Then I did get scared, thinking, "what are these guys going to do to me?" Well they didn't do anything except to give me a good scare and make me drop my bedtime meditations for a bit.

I know why they showed up too. It's because right before that I made a special prayer that was very important to me, it was only my second 'official' prayer, or request to the spirit world, and I still had a lot to learn.

This prayer I made was a big deal for me, and its focus was on saving the environment. It came about as a result of the presidential election where the anti-environmental winner clearly cheated. Before that there had been some hope that the environmental movement would help to reverse the downward spiral which manifests as the fastest extinction event in the history of the planet. It was getting bad then and not it's going full steam. It breaks my heart to see it.

It boils down to human overpopulation versus the animal kingdom, and in general I like animals more than people. So, my big prayer was about saving the environment, and the solution to the plan could involve me not living through it. So to put it another way, I was making a prayer that was risking my life in order to save nature and the animal kingdom. Something like that, coming from a well energized wizard's apprentice, tends to get the attention of some heavy hitters in the spirit realm, because I addressed most of them anyway.

This was the first real serious prayer I have made in my life and so I was a beginner at over age fifty. I had read about praying, and from my exposure to Taoism I knew, in order for it to have the best chance of success, it needed to be done with the highest ethical considerations. It took me a couple of weeks to work out the details of the ethics and come up with the best solution. I also figured it was standard practice to address some powerful being with the request, but I didn't know who to pray to, I didn't know which ones were real or imaginary so I took kind of a shotgun approach and named a bunch of them. The list of greats that I ended up calling on went something like this: God, Buddha, Jesus, Lao Tzu, Quan Yin, Sai baba, Babaji, I knew that Sai Baba and Babaji were real, with a high likelihood Buddha and Jesus were real too. My mistake was that when I was done addressing them, the word 'demons' popped in right at the end of the list there, unanticipated by me since it wasn't in the script I had carefully prepared over those weeks.

Evidently none of the others that I addressed were inclined to answer or take any action, but the demons were. What I learned from that scary experience is that it is possible for people to call on demons for assistance. It turns out they aren't so picky, they're willing to help people, but the more powerful the better, of course. For them.

If you are powerful then they want to help because if they do, then you are in debt to them. Then when you die you get to spend quality time in their ranks. Of course who doesn't prefer people with power on their team? It's natural. The good guys like power too, of course, but they're more concerned about the kind of power that comes from ethical conduct, virtue, a vast subject.

You see, at the time I had no idea that I was a shaman with any kind of spiritual power, I didn't know that my spirit was of a dragon, nor did I know my guardian was a dragon, but I'm getting ahead of the story here again.

This episode with the prayer and the demons answering showed me that, of course, dragons can call on demons for assistance if they wish, it's simply something they never wish to do. Therefore, when I semi accidentally called them they got a fantastic, once in a million year, opportunity they just couldn't resist. They kept their distance though, because they're scared shitless of my guardian, the white dragon, who stands by my right side.

I didn't know the white dragon was my guardian or spirit guide. This is how I found out. The finding out took more than a decade.

One evening I was sitting in bed meditating with eyes closed when this dramatic and mysterious face appeared to me. The end of the nose was around three feet away from me, and since the creature had a bit of a long nose it put the head further back. It was roughly the size of a human head except longer and a bit wider, more round than a human head. You could say that that nose and jaw, which were closed, gave it a look a lot like one of the raptor dinosaurs, which had nose and jaws higher than they were wide when the jaws are closed, indicating big teeth and strong jaws. Imagine a big raptor dinosaur that has a bigger than human size head staring at you from only three feet away. It could be a thrilling experience for some people. The eyes that were looking at me were big and yellow and had round pupils that looking forward with binocular vision, unlike raptors, which had small eyes on the side of their heads. Eyes like owl eyes, or eagle eyes.

It was covered with small scales like a reptile or dinosaur and the color was off white. Keep in mind I was meditating in a darkened room, so the scene was not very brightly lit, but a bit gloomy, making the visitor a soft off white or a very light gray, silvery, color. The scales all around the lips, nostrils, and eyes were larger than the others, and were a soft violet color which blended with the light gray of the rest of it.

Those big yellow eyes with their big round pupils that were so close to mine were actually looking at me from a vast distance, not necessarily of space, but of race, experience, knowledge, and power.

One thing that stood out in a remarkable way was also an essential part of its being. It had a kind of frill on its head like some dinosaurs had and some reptiles have now. Picture an umbrella with its hard ribs and and soft fabric, it was basically like that, going around the top and sides of its head and opening to the back. This large frill it had was the same off-white color as the rest of its head, except for the ribs which served as the support framework for the fabric of skin, they had the same light violet coloring as the scales around the lips, eyes, and nostrils.

He was holding his frill about half way open, neither all the way open in threat nor all the way closed as in relaxed, just neutral, indicating alertness I would guess, and this being was nothing if not alert. What was remarkable about this frill was that it had no ending I could see, it just faded softly into the background gloom, like it was meshed in with the fabric of the universe. It also looked like a big impressive crown it was wearing. Wearing permanently. Without that big frill/crown it would have looked a lot like a Komodo Dragon in some ways, but more like your common garden variety raptor dinosaur, except for the rather large yellow eyes looking forwards, which were looking out at me from something which the raptor dinosaurs and Komodo Dragons do not have, which is a forehead.

The eyes looked steadily at me with neither friendship nor enmity, just completely neutral, and so calm! It radiated a feeling of great wisdom and experience and an immense age. The calmness which emanated from its being and its eyes was astounding in its depth. I could tell from looking into its eyes that it was extremely, outstandingly, absolutely calm; a kind of calmness so severe, that I'm sure it would scare some people. Needless to say, it was expressionless. I knew that this great calmness came from having a great deal of power, I didn't know what kind of power that might be, like the power of a ruler, social power, power over life and death, but it was obviously a very powerful being.

It left after about seven seconds and I continued meditating, ignoring it like my teacher told me to, to ignore the visitors, and later I forgot about it.

I did think about it from time to time though, and since I knew there were no such things as dragons I assumed my scaly visitor must be either an intelligent dinosaur or an alien, and that it was just a random visit, meaningless.

In retrospect, during that time, as I grew into this path of the wizard, I had become curious about who my spirit guide or guardian might be. There were some indicators about it that I had missed. I did not occur to me that this dinosaur had come to see me was my spirit guide, and in any case it was just a mild curiosity I had.

Once, a student of mine who came to me to become an energy healer talked me into going to a big psychic fair in a giant room at the Boeing Aircraft Renton facility. I wandered around and looked at all the crystals and new age stuff, then as I passed by one of the psychics I had the whim to ask him who my spirit guide was, so I sat across from him at his little card table. It really was a card table, because he was using Tarot cards. I asked my question, then he shuffled the cards and did the Tarot thing. Once all the cards were turned over he looked up over my right shoulder for a couple of seconds and then said: "Don't be so eager to get to know your spirit guide because Satan will try to trick you." Then he said: "He will try much harder to get you, because if he does it will big a big coup for him."

So evidently this psychic had seen my guardian and assumed it was Satan.

As I left the table he lit a candle and started praying fervently.

I thought it was neat that Satan would try so hard to get me, it was good for my ego, verifying that I was one of the good guys.

About a year after this being visited me, I began thinking about it more and more, and decided to go see Mr. Yueng about it. I had planned to go one afternoon but when the afternoon arrived I got cold feet. I hadn't seen him in a couple of years and I didn't want to bother him with dumb questions, or bother him at all for that matter, so that afternoon I took a nap instead. While I was asleep he appeared to me in a dream and said: "You come tomorrow three o'clock!" So that was that. I went the next afternoon to see him at three.

I had drawn a rough front view sketch of the being that came to see me and showed it to him. Of course he knew all about it as he knew everything I was doing and thinking at home. He knew everything that happened to me. He never said, "I know what you thought/did." He would just casually comment on what I had done or thought in ways that left no doubt.

Anyway, I showed him the sketch and I, thinking there may have been a race of intelligent dinosaurs in the past, asked him if it was a dinosaur. He said no. So I asked if it was an Alien and he said no again. So I sat there for a few seconds pondering what it could have been and then he said: "It's an immortal." I couldn't think of anything to say to that, it's maybe a problem I have, which is a failure to ask questions at the best time. You could say it's simply unquestioning acceptance of statements, or you could say it's a serious case of lack of curiosity, or super slow curiosity. Anyway, there was no further discussion about my visitor, it didn't really mean anything to me at the time or for a long time after that. I wonder, if I had been wise enough to ask more, would he have told me what kind of immortal it was, what it meant, and why it came to see me? In any case it was much better that I didn't ask and he didn't tell, because I would have had difficulty believing him.

We went on to discuss a few other things, like me returning to have a picture taken of us together before I relocated to Ecuador. What he did tell me at the end was to only pray to one god and not a bunch of them, so I asked him which one and he suggested that I pray to Quan Yin, the Goddess of Compassion.

A year or so later, while on adventures with an Indian friend I went to see this American Indian shaman, who was very open and with such a pure heart, a joyous and advanced spirit. We went to his little cabin in the woods and during the ceremony I saw at one point he looked up over my head and saw something that impressed him a bit. He didn't say anything, but what I read from his brief and slight expression was that he had seen something that was a bit thrilling and powerful/dangerous at the same time. I also got the feeling he saw something which was watching over me.

A year or so after that, I went to be a student of a Hawaiian kahuna. I had been going to some self defense classes taught by one of my kung fu brothers named Tom. He is a well known top dentist, and sometimes people would fly half way across the world in their Lear jets in order to see him. He was one of the more able fighters in the world. Tom was the top student of my kung fu teacher, Dave, so when Dave passed away Tom took over the teaching duties. Tom liked to live on the wild side. He made friends with and got himself invited to visit one of the big mafia dudes in Seattle, and at one point he beat the hell out of the guy's best bodyguards, all friendly of course. He told me I should go see this kahuna friend of his if I wanted to see some real magic. I thought it would be great to see some magic, so I went to be a student of this kahuna.

He was 100% Hawaiian, he came from a family lineage of kahunas, and had been trained in the kahuna arts by his grandmother. He was internationally recognized as the most powerful kahuna in the Pacific Ocean. I went to see him monthly for around half a year or so and it became evident that he had a strong resentment against what the whites had done to the Hawaiians. He told us about how Christian missionaries had written down the previously oral Hawaiian "bible." and of course they had screwed it up, interpreting things from the viewpoint of brainwashed fundamentalists. They effectively destroyed the true and original Hawaiian spirituality, and all the other kahunas in Hawaii, and I mean all of them in Hawaii, except for his family, were trained in this bastardized system of kahuna cultivation and because of that their power was weak. This kahuna, who shall remain nameless, carried a smoldering anger towards whites for destroying the indigenous religious and spiritual system of his land. The whites had done things like putting broken glass on the paths in order to make the Hawaiians wear shoes, and he really hated them for that. He hated that the whites used and abused Hawaiians as house maids and servants. He hated that Hawaiians had been diverted from their culture by Christianity and due to that, he had no Hawaiian students, only whites … casually interested, poisoned whites.

It truly is a sad thing to see the end of a line like his, with him not having any Hawaiian students he was seeing his tradition being lost to time. It not uncommon at all, much knowledge is being lost these days. The Native American Indian shaman I had visited at his cabin in the woods had the same problem, the Indians in his own village had been turned against him by Christian preachers, and except for one relative, he had only casually interested whites as students. However, he cried about it rather than becoming a hater like the Kahuna had. It was the same thing with Mr. Yueng, at first he only wanted to teach chi kung to Chinese people, but none were interested. Even a couple of years after I started with him he was so pissed off about it that once he said: "Chinese people STUPID!" He said they were only interested in chasing after the almighty dollar and didn't care about spiritual growth. But of course he did love China and Chinese people ... it gets complicated. Since he couldn't get any Chinese students to come for even one month he wasn't going to teach chi kung, but then he met me, and his wife talked him into teaching.

So you see, the effect of first the church, and now the culture it has generated, is active even these days, destroying the indigenous spirituality almost everywhere in the world that it reaches. Sadly, a lot of knowledge is being lost during these days of the Great Stupidification, which has now been going on for over a thousand years. The beginning of the Great Stupidification began, in my mind, with the burning of the Great Library in Alexandria, Egypt, by the early crusaders and the beginning of the dark ages.

Unfortunately the kahuna directed some of this anger at me. It might have been because by way of introduction I told him I had grown up in South America and that we had maids. Unfortunately, I say, because he seemed to relate my parents having maids in South America with the abuses the Hawaiians suffered as servants to the whites; although my parent's were always very kind and helpful to the servants. The main reason I had mentioned having maids to him was because our maids had helped to raise me, to feed and care for me. I had spent more time with them than with my parents so in a way I was raised by poor South American Indians rather than white middle class Americans, which is what I was trying to tell the kahuna, but that backfired.

I and my two friends/students who joined me for his classes noticed that his long term students were strangely subdued and non-vibrant. It occurred to us there may have been some kind of energy vampirism going on there. It slowly dawned on me that the Kahuna took a powerful dislike to me, in the manner that someone with a poisoned heart will automatically despise someone with a pure heart.

He was also annoyed with me being so naive about my own spiritual progress and power; at one point he commented about me: "You're SO lucky," but he said it in a hissing angry jealous manner. He was verbally abusive to me often enough and I suspect he wanted me to not return, but I'm tough in some ways and will put up with some abuse in order to learn. This Kahuna was very powerful indeed. He had a lot of Chi power that he could blast you with, he could see your organs and what you were doing at home, and he could take you to Hawaiian hell. He took a couple of people, separately, on a psychic tour of Hawaiian hell, and when they returned one of them cowered in the fetal position for a couple of hours ... but I'll bet the kahuna couldn't take you to Hawaiian heaven!

At one point twelve of the Christianized kahunas in Hawaii got together and as a group sent a death spell to him. He simply turned it around and sent it back to the twelve kahunas. All of them died in a matter of a couple of days. My kung fu brother, Tom, who had sent me and who was friend with the kahuna, verified this to me, that he had become psychically aware of it as soon as it happened. Tom asked the kahuna if it was really necessary to kill all those guys because he knew some of them. He was told it had already been done and there was nothing that could be done about it. Those twelve guys got a taste of their own medicine, that is all. The kahuna spent a considerable amount of his time astrally visiting the spirit realm and joining in the never ending wars there, and my kung fu brother, Tom, was aware of this and joined him at times. Keep in mind that these wars in the spirit realm are all middle management stuff, the higher ups don't normally get involved.

So what does all this about the Kahuna have to do with my dragon guardian? It was during my last class as his student that he informed us he would go around the room - there were seven of us - and tell us each who our guardians were. I got exited about that! We were sitting on the floor and reclining against the wall of his basement as usual. He went around the room describing the people's various guardians in considerable detail. When he got to me, he said my guardian was a little old lady with a cloud of white hair who ignored me most of the time and was gone a lot! Well that was a let down. I was hoping for something with a little more oomph, although later I rationalized it, figuring that little old ladies with white hair can have a lot of wisdom.

Well I didn't know it then, but it turns out he was describing, and insulting, the immortal, that off-white colored reptile like being that had come to see me. The big white frill he had described as a cloud of white hair, and calling a dragon a little old lady could be correct in way, correct but quite misleading. It is old, yes, very old, and I don't know if it is male or female. The kahuna was lying to me, misleading me and putting me down, as was his nature. His big mistake though, is he pissed off the dragon, something he wanted to do on purpose. The kahuna was a warrior, after all.

He was a middle aged guy, younger than me, and in good health but shortly after that he died suddenly. I heard through the grapevine that some of his students said he had died in a psychic battle with some very dangerously powerful spirit that was trying to invade our dimension so to speak. Some months later I realized he had fought my guardian and that's how he died. Of course, the white dragon was pissed about being insulted and about me being misled, and the kahuna had challenged it directly. I found out through another very experienced old friend that this is not unheard of, he told me of two acquaintances of his who had both challenged dragons and who had both died for it soon thereafter.

Keep in mind I still did not believe in dragons, but I was getting the idea that this white reptile-looking immortal was my guardian. It seems I knew it subconsciously, and it slowly oozed into my conscious.

Not so long after my adventure with the kahuna I got old enough to qualify for social security, so I closed my business, cashed out my property and bank account, and moved to Southern Ecuador to build a new life in a pure land with a twelve month growing season. I had contemplated buying a catamaran and sailing around the Pacific, ending up in New Zealand, selling the boat and using that money to buy some land there. However when I mentioned that idea to Mr. Yueng he said that was too dangerous, so I skipped it.

After moving here to southern Ecuador I found this wonderful land to buy, land where no one had lived since the Incas. I lived alone in a little ten foot by ten foot wood shed while the house was being built, and I think that was the best time of my life; living like a hermit in a small wood shed, with only a few minutes of electricity a day from a noisy generator, almost no internet, and walking to the spring with a plastic bottle in order to get water. The boards my shack was made from shrank a lot when they dried so there are gaps between them. You can see out through the gaps and with the door and windows closed the wind blows right in so that sometimes the wind chimes make their sweet music even when it's all closed up. In fact I'm sitting here in the shed right now writing this book.

One evening I was sitting here in the shed and I focussed on this white visitor and asked it a question: "Are you an alien?" Right away the answer came back, a long drawn out "noooo." Then I asked: "Then what are you?" and again the answer came right back: "We are dragons."

For some reason I wasn't surprised, but it did give me a little thrill to know that dragons did exist and I had been wrong. What a wonderful fabulous mystery the universe is, isn't it? I love it! Dragons exist, at least in the spirit realm. The spirit realm is populated with immortals, dragons, demons, hungry ghosts, maybe the variety is endless. Due to this I try, as much as possible, to not have any beliefs as to what is not possible when it comes to the spirit world. It is vast, and apparently filled with wars here and there in case someone wants to get involved. It's just like the real world with all its little non stop wars and occasional big ones.

The voice of this dragon was markedly different from the few other communications I've had from the other side of the veil. It was slow speech but it was overlain with a fast wavering or fluttering sound, very much like ululating speech, but like it was far far away, reaching across a vast distance. Ululating as done in African tribal singing is done with high pitched voices but this dragon spoke in rather a kind of hissing low pitch - "We are dragons." Cool! There's so much I have learned each time from even the briefest contact with an immortal. I also learned that a Taoist immortal can become a dragon when they join the sky realm.

Later I focussed on the word "We". I had asked him the question in the singular, "what are YOU?" He responded, "WE are dragons." I asked him in the singular and he answered in the plural. At first I assumed that he was talking about his family. Later I realized that he was telling me I was a part of the family. Realizations come from have a super energized crown point, you find you know things without knowing why or how you know them. Such things are easily confused with having a wild imagination but the uninitiated, but there is nothing that can be done about that. You know, you have to have been there. He was telling me I was a dragon. Learning more about yourself is always great but can be confusing.

Anyway, hearing it from the dragon was a lot more convincing, nay, certain, than it would have been if I'd heard it from a person, even one like my teacher. If a person that I had absolute trust in had told me that I was a dragon then I would either ignore it, or assume they meant it in a symbolic fashion only. Hearing it from an actual dragon, however, made it clear. It is not symbolic, it is real, at least as real as something from the spirit realm can be, which from some points of view is more real than the 'real' world. I have discovered that in my lineage the masters body's and those of some students are inhabited by the spirits of dragons. Bruce Lee was called "Little Dragon" for more reasons than one. Mr. Yueng could be the white dragon. I know he was is immortal and he is or was a dragon too, I just don't know if he was that particular white dragon that came to see me. I think he may not be a dragon anymore, as he appears to have graduated past even that.

About a year after that, I was teaching some chi

kung in the town of Vilcabamba which is about fourteen miles away from our mountain fortress. It is a town in which many foreigners live. At one point this French guy who was a student came up to me and told me he'd had a dream about a dragon. I had not told him and did not tell him about my experience with dragons so it was out of the blue. He said he had dreamed about a dragon coming to town and that he wasn't afraid of it. So I asked him what color it was and he said it was black.

Later I did some research on Chinese dragons and their colors and discovered that the description of the character of the black dragon matched me perfectly. The black dragon is also associated with the dark warrior or mystic warrior, and I didn't know till I researched it, that my favorite T shirt, one I loved and wore all the time, had the mystic warrior emblem on it. So for years I had been parading around wearing 'my' emblem without knowing it. The emblem of the dark warrior is the intertwined turtle and snake. These things are just further verification to me about the correctness of the knowledge.

At one point a very psychic Russian lady channeler came to visit me here on the mountain and she told me there were dragons in the mountains around here, that they were happy I am here, and they will help to protect me. The main thing they want is for me to take good care of the land. I have planted around 9000 native forest trees to refor-est what was previously some steep cattle grazing land. Since then several other people who have come out here to visit have commented that they sensed dragons around.

Sometimes I wonder, how is it possible for a per-son to be a human being and a dragon at the same time? My best guess, supported by some evidence from earlier in life, is that I'm a reincarnation of a black dragon and my spirit is that of a black dragon, perhaps a baby one. I don't really know, and I don't really care, all will be revealed in due time.

Steve Smith, my kung fu brother and fearless clan leader who is the designated inheritor of Mr. Yueng's self defense system, has been visited by dragon of three different colors. I'm guessing that he is also a dragon.

My research into the colors of dragons revealed more.

For example, the white dragon, my guardian, is very yang. White is the most yang, both of colors and of dragons, the boldest, the most powerful, representing the fullness of development of its abilities. After fullness then waning appears. A bright white dragon represents the peak of yang, but my guardian, the pale off-white dragon, is so ancient that its brightness is fading it is ready for the next step. The literature explains that the main job of the pale off-white dragon is to serve as Grim Reaper for Taoists. It is said that when the pale white dragon comes to visit a practitioner of the Way it means that the person will die soon, but he came to see me and I didn't die.

Imagine that, to have the Grim Reaper as your personal guardian. Why do you suppose I have such a powerful guardian? The white dragon isn't guarding me so much as it's guarding the spiritual path for dragons on Earth, which is Mr. Yueng's version of Tien Shan Chi Kung, and since I'm a holder of this wondrous thing, and been bestowed with the burden of sharing it with others, then I need a little help in the spiritual safety department.

To give you an idea of how this guardian stuff works: Nate and Chris are a couple of guys who came down here to practice some chi kung. Nate had been here earlier working as a volunteer and he liked the chi kung so much he told his friend Chris about it. Chris started practicing the chi kung that Nate showed him and he became quite psychic, he started to see and hear from dead people, which he didn't really like. The two buddies came down together to visit for awhile and practice some chi kung and kung fu. One evening Chris noticed that there was a spirit standing behind me. I'll just share what he said using his own words:

"One startling realization took hold, I realized my

ability to move objects was diminished here, but another form of energy, or rather, ability started to make its presence known by the third night. We were finishing up our standing meditation at around 9 p.m. and about to do our 30 minutes seated when I saw a shadow that had no source begin to take form behind Steve. Its characteristics began to come more and more into focus and I could see it was a bald man in a monk's robes with prayer beads in his hand staring at Steve with a very sinister expression. I even interrupted our meditation session to point out where the shadow figure was standing, and I was in complete disbelief of what I was seeing. Once I moved closer to him he vanished and reappeared crouching up in the back corner of the Dojo. Every time I stared at the man the only thoughts that came to my head were of anger and a hostile feeling of wanting to hurt Steve which came from this presence."

The idea that some unfriendly spirit was doing something to me or was even in the room was upsetting. I directed my attention to the white dragon, and in my head I told him: "Hey, are you seeing this? Aren't you supposed to be doing something about this?"

Later someone with a great deal of experience in these things told me that sometimes some malicious spirits will impersonate monks, and that they give people cancer. The following evening the bad boy in the monk's robes was not there.

Chris didn't see the monk, but he did see the white dragon that dark night with its brightly shining fog of stars. He said it appeared to be made of stardust, and it came in with a boom. The dragon told him: "I am of stars, I am with Steve." and Chris told me about seeing the white dragon, before I told him I had called it.

It's like the old and powerful white dragon, having reached the fullness of its growth and power, is going on to the next stage of his evolution. My guardian is preparing to transition to the next step, and so is bringing along a new little black dragon. Black represents the newness and the nothingness that precedes the unfoldment of anything. There is an unwritten law which says a master must share his knowledge with at least one other person before they die, so it seems likely the same thing goes on with dragons in the spirit realm. Unfortunately in this modern age that, law is being broken quite a lot. Hopefully there is a little dragon out there somewhere that would like to learn the spiritual path of the dragons from me before I kick the bucket. However, dreaming on, I can see how I may someday be teaching this system of cultivation to real dragons. I imagine they would be damn good students, and by good I mean they are dedicated and learn well and quickly.

The color of the black dragon represents yin, and I certainly am a yin person. I researched it and was amazed to find that the characteristics of Asian black dragons, as reported in the literature, match my character very well. The black dragon is the most yin of all. The black dragon is extremely yielding physically, mentally, and emotionally. He avoids crowds and publicity and prefers to stay in the background. He can be wishy washy and indecisive, since he feels that no choice is often better than some choice; or as Lao Tzu put it in the Tao Te Ching: "The sage has no mind of his own, his mind is the people's mind." So yin and yielding is the key, he tends to go along with what others want and doesn't care about much for himself.

Dragons are said to be naive in the fashion of a person with a pure heart, and what they want more than anything is the preservation of nature. As you can see, human overpopulation is interfering with what dragons want, so there is space there already for some animosity between humans and dragons.

The black dragon is the mystic, the alchemist, the sorcerer. They represent the vast emptiness which is un-manifested potential fullness of any and all abilities, so they usually do well in whichever venture they put their hand to. The opposite side of that coin is that they feel like they represent a lot of wasted talent. The black dragon is known for its power and revenge, although to him revenge doesn't look so much like revenge as it looks like punishment. If someone does you wrong, should they be punished for it? Should you be the punisher? It's up to you to decide the answer to those questions for yourself.

In China the dragons are considered to have potent and auspicious powers, particularly control over the weather. in the spirit realm at least some if not all dragons are human immortals. In the culture, excellent and outstanding people are said to be like dragons. These people, who are compared to dragons, if they dedicate themselves to the right path, may someday become immortals and real dragons when they evaporate away from their human cocoon. Off into the spirit realm they go, a place that is unreal for the inexperienced and yet real for the experienced.

The reason that European dragons have gotten such a bad rap is due to the workings of the church. The church did everything possible to destroy the indigenous spirituality of Europe when they were taking over, and they did an outstanding job of it. Since dragons really do exist in the spirit realm the European shamans would have naturally been aware of them and perhaps had some dealings with them. Dragons are known to be guardians, and the church had no use for spiritual guardians which did not like them. Dragons are ethical and essentially friendly if they are treated with kindness, but if people are bad to them they can be bad right back. Perhaps this helps to explain this old outdated Teutonic view of dragons. It was the darkness that was trained into people during the dark ages, it seems there was so much that was considered evil back then, like cats, women, paganism, you name it; if it didn't put more money in the church coffers it was an enemy.

I recently saw a passage in the bible about dragons. Evidently the power hungry and money hungry clowns that rewrote the bible for their own benefit added a passage which says that dragons are Satan. Well I can understand that, dragons must have been the biggest enemies of the oh-so-evil church for them to be labeled as the church's biggest enemy. In order to give you an idea of how I look at it: What do you call the biggest enemy of one of the most evil entities on Earth? This bible passage about dragons explains why the psychic who saw my guardian thought it was Satan; he had been well indoctrinated into Churchianity.

The Chinese Dragon is also the holder of the Pearl. You've probably seen Chinese paintings of dragons holding a pearl. The pearl is the Pearl of Immortality, and dragons are the guardian of it. According to the many myths and folk stories, it takes a brave and adventurous lad to go find a dragon and take the pearl from him. If he is good at heart and makes friends with the dragon, it takes him for a fantastic sightseeing ride flying around the world. The flying around with the dragon, and sight seeing, symbolizes a student's initiation into the family of dragons and pearl holders.

Keep in mind that these dragons exist in the spirit realm, which is why it is commonly easier for those with psychic sight to see them with their eyes closed rather than open. I don't know if a dragon can manifest a physical body. Some immortals can incarnate, but I don't know if dragons can. I assume that if a dragon did manifest a physical body that it would probably take on a human form similar to the one they had when they were people. For a person to have the spirit of a dragon animating them is not the same thing.

5 - THE EARLY YEARS

I didn't last long at the university. I thought it would be good to get a part time job so for my second quarter I arranged for all my classes to be early in the morning which gave me time in the afternoons to work. However I got turned on to pot during the first quarter, so what I did during the second quarter was partying at night and then sleeping in and missing all my morning classes, then going to work in the afternoon. I was working at a tire retreading facility and was in charge of running the pin striping machines. I would cut a shallow groove in the tire in the sidewall, put in a strip of colored rubber, and then bake it in a vulcanizing machine. Back then it was easy to get a job anywhere, and the wages were good. Eight dollars an hour, which is minimum wage now, was worth so much more back then than it is today.

Due to missing all my classes I got awarded 'incomplete' for each class on my second quarter report card, and I didn't bother applying for the third quarter. I worked at the tire sho for a few months and then lost interest and retired from there.

Some of my pot smoking buddies were working as unskilled laborers at the shipyards, getting temporary jobs through the Ship Scalers Union. The union had been dominated by pot smoking African Americans, and so the infiltration of pot smoking hippies was well tolerated.

I ended up getting jobs through the Ship Scaler's Union. Getting ship scaler jobs through the union was an on and off proposition. We would get hired for a particular job on a particular ship, and then get laid off. So sometimes we worked two weeks and sometimes we worked two days before getting laid off, and back to the union hall we went. Sometimes there was no work for a couple of weeks or even a couple of months, and other times we would work pretty steadily for a few months. One week I worked four days, and got hired and laid off three different times that week.

So there was a lot of 'vacation' time involved with that kind of work. Which included the opportunity to collect unemployment quite often.

In my early twenties I went to a two day Mind Dynamics seminar which was developed by Alexander Everrett, who is known as the father of the human potential movement. It was taught by Tom Wilhite. For me it was a wild new experience in self hypnosis, meditation, and long distance psychic healing work. During one part we lay down on the floor next to a student who sat on the floor next to us and who had a card with someone's name on it. We were then given the name of that person who had some health problem who lived in another city. We were tasked with looking at and inside this person's body to determine what kind of health problem they had and then working to fix the problem, which included hand and arm movement while we lay on the carpeted floor. I did this with two different people and I felt terribly uncertain, like I was making it up, but was informed that in fact I had seen the problem correctly. Still, the feeling of uncertainty persisted because there was no self assurance that I was seeing correctly. At one point during the seminar the leader asked if anyone in the audience had a headache. Well I had a slight headache so when no one else raised their hand I raised my hand. Tom said: "we don't allow headaches here," so he came over and stood in front of me. He told me to close my eyes and tell him what my headache looked like, so I did and said it was a purple dot. So with my eyes still closed he put his finger on my forehead and counted to three. When he said one the purple dot went away, when he said two the headache went away, and when he said three I felt a big surge of warmth inside my head. Then he left. Feeling the big burst of warmth was amazing to me so I was sitting there with my mouth hanging open when a lady sitting three seats to the right leaned forward, looked over at me and said: "Well, did the headache go away?" I relied yes. That was the first experience I had with any kind of energy/spiritual/psychic healing work and I didn't have any more for a long time thereafter.

Following that, when I was in my late twenties, I went to another weekend seminar. It was titled Inward Bound and was taught by my first 'spiritual' teacher, who was a pompous old Englishman named Alexander Everett and who had been the teacher of Tom Wilhite, the leader of my Mind Dynamics seminar. Alexander was an expert in comparative religion and had recently spent a lot of time in India learning from various Hindu gurus and yogis. In this class we learned about the values of meditation, and meditated several times while sitting in our chairs. One of the meditations was guided meditation, and the others were no mind, non thinking meditations. I was new to meditation, and liked it.

One thing that made a key, long-lasting impression on me was something that Alexander talked about. He was telling us about the people who lived into their eighties. He said that the eighties are called a person's "golden years" because by eighty they've usually figured out how to live a good happy long life, they've learned how to relax and enjoy their remaining days. Remaining days are viewed as gold - who wants some gold? I can't recall the statistics he used way back then so I'll just make those up here in order to provide the example. He said by the time they get into their eighties that 45% had already passed away,

25% had to continue working in order to make ends meet, 15% were depending on their children for support, 8% were handicapped and were being supported by the government, 5% were independent and making ends meet on their retirement, and only 2% were in good physical and financial condition.

Then he said that those who weren't in those last two categories had essentially failed. Failed at life essentially, or that's how it struck me.

I decided right there that I wanted to be one of those top percenters which were financially independent as well as physically independent, with the accent on being in better shape than just independent, the accent was on being healthy and in good condition, able to enjoy life in my golden years. That goal which Alexander gifted me has been a leading motivator throughout my life, and it seemed to me that any intelligent person will realize the importance of focusing on their health, of giving it priority, and most important of all, the younger you are when you start doing it the better the results will be in later years. Young people don't think so much about those things though. It is a mark of maturity.

The older I get the more I feel lucky to have chosen health and longevity as my goals. I had, and still have, no interest in wealth. After all, the older you get the wiser you get, and this wisdom normally makes it easier to make a living at something you like, with the requirement being that you have enough health and vitality to do it. The older you get, if you are a man, the less competition you have for women, and the more likely those women are to be wealthy. So just take good care of yourself, both physically and emotionally, and the rest will take care of you. By this I mean, since the universe is kind to those who truly wish the best for others, if you are kind to yourself, and the universe is also kind to you, what could be better than that?

6 - SAI BABA

I guess the most important thing that happened during that Inward Bound seminar I had with Alexander is that he introduced me to Sai Baba. Alexander told us the story of how he met Sai Baba. One fine summer day he was walking down a street in San Fransisco in the Haight Ashbury district at the time when it was the Hippie capital of the world, and he saw a poster of Sai Baba, who he had not heard of at the time. He was struck by some strong energy on seeing the poster, and something compelled him to find out who it was, so he went in the shop and they told him.

Since Alexander was heavily into the Hindu system of spirituality he decided to go see Sai Baba and so went to India to the ashram. A Westerner who was there told Alexander he had no chance of talking with Sai Baba because he had not interviewed any Westerners for a couple of months. Alexander got there late, and the evening meditation was already in progress, so he went into the big meditation hall and sat in the back and started meditating. After sitting there for a little while he got an impulse to open his eyes and look over to the right. So he did, and there he saw Sai Baba standing in a doorway looking at him.

The next morning, with the aid of time zone difference, Alexander got up before it got light and was one of the first to made it to the meditation hall, so he sat front row center on the men's side of the big room, cross legged on the floor. As is traditional, the men sat on one side and the women sat on the other side. When Sai Baba came out to greet the audience Alexander whipped up his camera and took a picture. Then Sai Baba walked straight towards him and stood over him for a second, Alexander was worried that Sai Baba had come over because it was against the rules to take pictures but the guy sitting next to him kicked him a little and told him: "he wants you to come and talk with him." In all there were three people chosen to go into a back room with Baba so they could talk, and they were all Europeans. There was Alexander, who taught beginning spirituality in seminars, there was another guy who had built an apartment building somewhere, and an Italian doctor who had built a hospital.

Once they got to the room Sai Baba turned to Alexander and said: "What is your question?" Well, Alexander wasn't ready for this and didn't have the big question about life ready, so the only thing he could think of saying was, "why did you choose to talk to me today when you haven't interviewed any white people for two months?" Sai Baba answered: "Because I know what you do." Then Alexander said: "What do you mean?" So

Sai Baba started doing an imitation of Alexander during one of his seminars, including the pompous English accent and saying things that Alexander commonly said during the seminars. Then Sai Baba turned to each of the others and answered their questions.

Then he came to Alexander and said: "What do you want?" Once again, Alexander was taken by surprise, what popped into his mind was *vibhuti*, which are the holy ashes that people use to anoint themselves. Sai Baba was well known for materializing large amounts of it during some of his ceremonies. So Sai Baba said, somewhat impatiently: "Well hold out your hands!" Alexander whipped his hands out palm up, and Sai Baba put his hand above Alexander's in a sort of 'birds beak' tai chi hand position, and started rubbing his fingers together. A little stream of ashes fell into Alexander's hands until he had around a teaspoon of it. He didn't know what to do with it, so he put some on his tongue and some on his forehead.

Then Sai Baba turned to the apartment builder and I can't remember what that guy wanted, but when he came to the doctor, the doctor wanted a gold ring which is a gift that the master often gave to his visitors. So he stuck his hand out in front of the doctor's face, palm up, and started to make little circles with his hand. A gold ring materialized in his palm, it took a couple of seconds to become solid after first appearing in his palm as a shadow. He put the ring on the doctor's finger but it was too big and fell on the floor. Sai Baba said: "Oh, so sorry," then picked it up, held the ring between his thumb and forefinger, and blew through it twice. This time it fit perfectly.

Then it was time to go, and Sai Baba turned to Alexander and asked him if he wanted any *vibhuti* to take with him. Alexander said yes, and this time he snapped his hands out right away. Once again Sai Baba did the thing with rubbing his fingers together, but this time what came out were little flat packets of the ash, wrapped in a type of newsprint paper, with Sai Baba's picture on one side, and a little prayer in Hindi on the other side.

After telling us the story about his visit to the ashram Alexander showed us his wallet picture of Sai Baba. He had this little photograph in his wallet and got that out. Of course, a wallet sized picture is pretty small and I was sitting about in the middle of the room, back maybe like twenty five feet from where Alexander was sitting on the low stage. Due to this, I couldn't see the picture so well, but in spite of that I had a remarkable experience. I saw the picture glowing with a big yellow aura around it, and I felt love coming from the picture. No kidding, and that was the first time I ever felt love. In general I think that the only time a person can feel love is when they give it, not when they receive it, and I never did that before either, however here I was clearly receiving love from another, and it's something I've never felt before or since. It was a very nice feeling, this feeling of love. I wonder how I even knew that it was love, but I did know it. The last thing that happened is I knew I was looking at god in spite of being a devout atheist. Now the important thing here is to differentiate between the meanings of thinking and knowing. My belief that there is no god was thinking. The fact I was looking at god through that picture was a certainty, he made me do it, so to speak. Anyway, now that I've grown, up I'm agnostic. I don't waste any more energy on that beliefs crap. Sai Baba was an avatar, which means he was an incarnation of god, so in a way he was showing me how his system of spirituality worked. If you can love a god and feel the love back, then more power to you.

Imagine you had an interview with Sai Baba, got to ask your question and then choose your gift. If you had time to prepare for it, to decide what really is your one and only most important question, what would that question be? ...

If you had a chance to ask Sai Baba for a gift what would it be? What gift could be best for you? Which then begs the question: What could be best for you? What is your true goal? You need to have a firm idea of what's best for you if you're going to ask for some gift to help you get yourself along closer to your goal. So what would it be? Ten Cadillac cars? A million dollars?

Many of the people he sees ask him for something that they can keep with them, that they can wear all or most of the time, so this often took the form of a ring, but also sometimes of a nice watch.

In fact, once Sai Baba lamented that everybody asks for trinkets and no one asks him for what he is really here to give. I never asked him for it either, but he gave me a good taste of what he was here to give anyway some decades after the seminar, on the other side of the world.

Another thing that happened during that seminar is the guy sitting behind me tapped me on the shoulder and told me my aura was very big. Well I thought it was kind of neat but had no idea what to make of it. I assumed it was just me, but it could well be that my interaction with Sai Baba had energized me.

Some years later I was having coffee with a guy who was wearing a very big complex silver ring that looked like the figure of a seated person. I asked him about the ring and he said Sai Baba had materialized it for him during a private interview. I then told him about what I had experienced from seeing Sai Baba's picture and he told me that was quite rare and that I was clearly important or special to Sai Baba in some way.

Sai Baba was quite a controversial person and I can see he liked it that way. He was a tricky guy and liked to have a little fun while at the same time giving some viewers in the audience what they asked for. What he would do is sometimes perform a botched sleight of hand and appear to produce some trinket from underneath his seat cushion. Assuming he did take it from underneath his seat cushion, the question is whether or not he made the object materialize there first, before showing it. I'll share a couple of stories about him that I was told in person.

One time Sai Baba produced a Rolex watch in this way, which he gave to one of his fans. Rolex watches have serial numbers and can be traced ... so they traced it and found it was sold in a watch store in a different city in India from the one the gifting had been done in. The shop owner told them Sai Baba had come into his store and purchased the watch, and the interesting thing is that Sai Baba had purchased the watch at the same time as he was giving it as a gift, which means he had been in two places at once (called bi-locating, which is a popular thing for Hindu Avatars and saints to do).

Once a friend of mine named Michael went to see Sai Baba in India and told me about this other guy he met there who was called Buster. Buster was unsure if Sai Baba was for real or not so he told his wife that if Sai Baba was for real, he would see a rainbow that day. Sure enough, that afternoon there was a glorious double rainbow. Then, later in the afternoon, the couple happened to come across Sai Baba as he was walking through one of the courtyards and Sai Baba asked: "How'd you like the rainbow, Buster?" Buster flopped on the ground and started kissing his feet.

That's definitely not my style. I'm not a ground flopping, foot kissing kind of guy, even if they were god. I would rather say Hi and look into their eyes.

During the time Michael was there he also caught sight of Sai Baba walking through one of the court-yards, and he took many pictures. This was back when cameras used film. Michael took a whole roll of film of Sai Baba walking by. Later when he got back to the States he had the film developed and was surprised to see there were a couple of pictures of Sai Baba at the beginning, the whole middle of the roll was pictures of blue sky with white clouds in it, and there were a couple of pic-tures at the end of the roll that showed him walk-ing away.

What usually happened is that if Sai Baba was talking to someone in person in a private setting, then when he materialized something it would appear in the palm of his hand right in front of the recipient's face, taking a second or two to go from transparent to solid. If he was putting on a talk in front of a big audience then he was likely to take something, or appear to take something, from underneath his seat cushion. I guess that if some people were to see something materialize in front of their eyes and it was against their beliefs, it could cause irreparable emotional damage, so they were spared from that. At the same time Sai Baba was not so much into satisfying all the idly curious tourists who came to see him do a circus act rather than to hear his message.

Sai Baba has now passed away, but his spirit is still active among his followers.

7 - MEETING THE MASTER

Possibly you are the kind of person who likes to read books about great masters of the Far East. I was. I was enchanted to get a glimpse of the lives and abilities of some of the great hidden masters, and what impressed me often was to read about the amazing psychic abilities and synchronicity that they lived with. I thought it would be very cool to be one of those few lucky students of those few hidden masters, but it was kind of a far off dream. I wouldn't possibly know where to start looking for such a master, and I didn't really have the finances to travel like that either, wandering around, looking for who knows what, and it's a good thing I didn't go anyway. The chances of finding such a master would be slim at best, essentially impossible to be practical, because by then in India and the Himalayas they had discovered the magic of tourist dollars, so most had changed gears to accommodate the quick 'n' easy types of students.

This was back before the internet, and you couldn't just look up any information about any subject you were interested in. So with no money for travel and getting caught up in the work force; with no knowledge of any specific place to go, I forgot about that dream and settled down as best I could, which was not so good really, into the rat race.

However I did end up meeting one of these top masters after all, because as it turns out, some of the most advanced ones very quietly moved to the West. A few of these great masters left their home country and came to America and Europe, the really advanced ones shun popularity like the plague, and like to stay hidden. They didn't come to the West to suck money out of any and every student that crossed their path. They saw the writing on the wall and escaped from their homeland before the Cultural Revolution, which is when the Red Brigade went all around China and Mongolia killing, imprisoning, and torturing masters of all sorts.

I became interested in life energy (chi), towards the end of my thirties. I don't know why, because I hadn't been reading about it much that I recall, I was really into reading science fiction at the time, so I suspect it was my past life spiritual path resurfacing.

Right around when I turned forty I went looking for a teacher so that I could learn about this strange energy, and for some reason I went to martial arts training in order to learn it. More past life stuff resurfacing. I found an Aikido master in Everett, Washington, not so far from where I was living, which was about half way from Seattle to Everett. I think he was Irish. The curious thing is that this teacher had some good strong Jedi type abilities, and he liked to play around with them in class with his senior students. I say curious because firstly, for a teacher to have these kinds of abilities is rare and I stumbled across one on my first try, plus this was a preview of my future as well as being even more connected to past life abilities resurfacing. For the rest of this book, when I speak of Jedi abilities or Jedi stuff I am referring to the ability to push someone with energy or otherwise control their movements with energy or mind control ... that is to say, without touching them.

The Jedi stuff this Aikido master did with his students was interesting to watch, but it's what he did without knowing it that was the clincher for me. One time he and a senior student were standing back to back, but without touching. Each of them was talking to a student that was standing in front of them. The teacher started to demonstrate something and started twisting back and forth, and the student he had his back to started twisting in unison with him, as if they were meshed together at the waist with gears, yet without touching and without paying any attention to it. The training was basic beginning Aikido which consisted of some different strengthening exercises plus practicing rolling, falling, and tumbling along with some simple self defense techniques. Aikido didn't interest me so much, and at one point while tumbling I did it wrongly and instead of doing a nice roll I ended up crashing down on my right shoulder and hurting it, which forced me to stop going to classes. The shoulder got better but I stayed stopped.

Several years later one of this Aikido master's students came to be my chi kung student for a while. The teacher used to do a considerable amount of what appeared to be Jedi stuff to this young man when I was in class and he was just a teenager. He told me that what was really happening was that he was responding to threat gestures. He said that if he didn't respond in the correct manner the teacher would hurt him. A threat gesture is a technique used, like the beginning of a punch, for example, but without following through with it. Threat gestures can work well as tricks, to get an opponent to move in a certain way that sets them up for a different technique. Simply put, you threaten to punch someone in the face so they duck, simple. The thing here is that a threat gesture can look just like a Jedi type energy push. In fact, for those who have trained and are sensitive to energy, yielding away from incoming energy is a desired reaction. Details.

Next, I got a little closer to my roots. I decided I wanted to learn tai chi, and through the yellow pages found a tai chi school taught by a kung fu master in Chinatown, so I went to watch a class. It was in a big old dirty, dark, and dreary upstairs warehouse room. When I got there I sat on a wood bench near to the door and watched. There were only two students in the large room. They were standing up against the wall on one side and each of them had an instructor standing in front of him. They were doing some kind of simple exercise like lifting one leg and moving the knee in a circle, and then the other, some kind of balancing exercise. The master only showed up to shake my hand when I came in, then he went back into the other room and ignored the students and their teachers. The whole thing was kind of dark and uninviting to say the least. I never went back.

Many years later I found out this teacher was a fake master. He went to China for a couple of months and took some kung fu lessons. When he got back to Seattle he opened a school and called himself a kung fu master. He actually had the nerve to send Mr. Yueng a letter challenging him to a fight. Mr. Yueng gladly accepted the challenge, and replied he would be at the guy's dojo at a certain date and time, but when he arrived the fake master was no-where to be found. So Mr. Yueng bought one of their T shirts from the downstairs store as a trophy.

This master was good at one thing, he knew how to do the trick that you may have seen, where someone puts a spear against the base of their throat and then leans on it in order to bend the spear. Once he did a public demonstration of that at a big event which Tai Chi Grand master Tchoung Ta Tchen happened to be attending. When Tchoung saw the spear trick he went over and said: "You are strong there, but what about here?" and grabbed a big handful of the guy's side and pinched hard. Mr. Fake Master fell on the floor in agony.

This is related to something relatively unknown, that the old time tai chi masters could do. They could grab someone hard on each side of their belly, by their love handles, so to speak, in a really hard pinch that could crush organs, then shake the person in a hard twisting motion that was violent enough to kill them, like a dog shaking a rabbit and killing it by breaking its back.

Shortly after that, I was walking through Woodland Park in North Seattle one bright sunny afternoon and I saw two guys practicing some kind of self defense stuff so I walked over and asked them about that teacher in Chinatown. They were polite enough about it but it was clear they considered that to learn anything from that guy would be a big mistake.

It turned out one of those guys, Andy Dale, was a tai chi teacher, and he gave me his business card. Years later I discovered that he was one of the more advanced Caucasian tai chi teachers one could hope to meet and a true master of the art.

Mr. Yueng told me that Andy was a master, and he would know. The other guy was Dave Harris, he was in the top 0.01% of the best of the best fighters in the world. Dave was the number one adopted son of Mr. Yueng, and Andy was his second adopted son. It's amazing how quickly I gravitated towards my lineage once my interest got switched on. I was a dragon, which I didn't know at the time, and then when I began looking for my teacher I accidentally ran into two other dragons who were to be my brothers and teachers, while they were playing in the park.

About a month after meeting Andy I decided to visit one of his classes. I liked what I saw. It was a huge contrast to the tai chi class I had seen in Chinatown. It was a cozy brightly lit space with carpeting on the floor. The students were clearly having fun learning, and Andy kept everyone learning as fast as they could. He was a good teacher and the class had a bright and exciting energy to it. I signed up for his Yang Tai Chi classes, which were on Tuesday mornings.

I loved tai chi because it required so much concentration, careful observation and careful imitation, which were actually new and challenging activities which I really enjoyed learning to develop. It was the first time in my life I had ever tried learning anything which was a real challenge, and I loved it. Everything I had learned in school or on the job had always been too easy. I promptly entered a world I hadn't even known existed ... a world of meditational movement. Since tai chi has so many rules to focus on and movements and postures to get just right it occupied my mind more than anything ever before. I found out tai chi is one of the best types of meditation that a beginner could hope to start with. I also found out tai chi is plenty of exercise, and except for a little hiking, I had never exercised before that. All the exercise I had previously known about was just so boring and mindless I couldn't get into it. Tai chi, though, was just as much training for the mind as it was for the body, plus it trained balance and coordination, and it even trained a person in fighting. The most important thing though, is I really liked it, and enjoyed practicing so much that I did very well, so much so that after a couple of years Andy recommended I start teaching tai chi.

Around that time, on a glorious Seattle summer evening I was in Woodland Park watching Andy leading a class in Chen Tai Chi . That class was a small one and all the students were pretty advanced. Many of them were also teachers. I wasn't learning Chen style at the time, so I just sat on the ground, leaned back against a big evergreen tree and watched.

I was there because it was Andy's birthday, and after class we all went to a local Greek restaurant to celebrate. There were about twenty of us, and we ended up sitting at one long table. Sitting across the table from me and one chair over, was an older Chinese man I had seen standing around outside the restaurant. He was very polite and seemed a little shy. Most of us were wearing jeans and sweatshirts and that sort of thing, with the women being typically a little better dressed than the men. But he was wearing a very nice new looking dark blue business suit with a very bright white shirt and tie.

Next to him was a young Chinese woman, Angela, who was acting as his translator. We started talking about Chi Kung and she told me that he was a Chi Kung master. I mentioned that I was learning a type of Chi Kung called Iron Shirt from a book and that I wanted to teach Chi Kung. She wasn't able to translate Iron Shirt style in a way that he understood, so I went to the head of the table and asked Andy, the birthday boy, how I should describe it. He told me and then he said: "He's the most advanced Kung Fu master on the West Coast. He was Bruce Lee's Kung Fu teacher." Then I was a bit in awe. I thought it was very cool to be sitting right across from a real master, and not just any master, but a really advanced kung fu master. He even gave me his card. It said "Master in Chi Kung" on it, and his name, Fook Yueng. He traded places with Angela so that he was sitting right across from me, then he ut his hands on my elbows for a couple of seconds. Then he got up and checked my shoulders, then he put his hands on a few places on the back of my neck. He told me I had some blockages in my neck. For people to have blockages in their neck is not uncommon, but I had a bad one, and didn't know it.

That evening while at the restaurant he did some interesting things. He put his hand on the wrist of the guy sitting next to him and after a couple of seconds said, "Oh, you hurt your knee." He was right. About a year earlier the guy in question, Bruce, had slipped on wet grass while practicing Tai Chi in the park, and had suffered a serious knee injury. Later during that dinner Mr. Yueng made a fist and had one of the other guys put his palm over it, this person then exclaimed "WOW!" I had no idea what was going on there, but in retrospect I'll bet he got a big blast of energy into his hand.

Later, in morning Tai Chi class, Andy told me he noticed Mr. Yueng had been playing around at making people move unconsciously, as if they were puppets, as if he was pulling their strings. He also told me a little about Mr. Yueng and Bruce Lee.

Meeting Mr. Yueng and getting his card made a real big impression on me, more, for example, than meeting the president of the United States would have. Later Andy told me in private that Mr. Yueng was accepting students, and I had no idea he meant me, at the time, and it took me a month or two to build up the nerve to tell Angela that I wanted to be Mr. Yueng's student. Years later I was told tit was Angela who talked him into teaching Chi Kung because at first he wasn't going to teach Westerners.

Angela went to Andy's Yang Tai Chi class, so she was my Tai Chi sister. I still thought Iron Shirt Chi Kung from the popular book by Mantak Chia was a good thing, so at one point I gave his book on Iron Shirt to her so Mr. Yueng could look at it. She brought the book back the following week and told me Mr. Yueng said it was a bunch of unrelated stuff someone had thrown together. Since Mr. Yueng was super psychic he would have known that for me to have become a student of and teacher for that guy would be like throwing me in the trash. I guess they didn't like the idea of throwing me to the dogs like that.

At that time Angela was walking about fifteen blocks north to get to a bus stop so I offered to give her a ride and she accepted, but I could tell she was concerned I was trying to pick her up so I told her about my being recently married and also having recently adopted a little girl. On the way up there and after arriving at the bus stop we talked for a while about Chi Kung and Mr. Yueng. I said it would be great if I could take lessons from him and she said I should pay him a visit. The following week I gave her a ride to the bus stop again. This time she told me Mr. Yueng wanted to see me, so I gave her my phone number. She called me a few days later and we made an appointment to see Mr. Yueng. I was worried that after checking me out, he would find me unacceptable for some reason.

On my first visit to Mr. Yueng I was nervous. I had the fear of rejection, plus I didn't know how to act. I showed up at his front door at the appointed time and rang the doorbell. After a couple of minutes that seemed like a very long time he opened the front door and brought me back into his garage. Mr. Yueng is such a gentle person that I soon relaxed. Besides, he told me to sit in a chair and relax.

He sat in a chair facing me. He had me put my hands in my lap palms up and then put his hand about a foot above mine and slowly opened his hand up with his palm facing down towards my hands. He made slight up and down and side to side motions like he was feeling something. Then he stood up and started going over my arms, shoulders, chest and back in the same way. He said I had pain in my chest muscles and he was right. The previous week I had done a hard isometric chest exercise and had strained my chest muscles. They had been sore for several days, but by that time the soreness was almost gone. He asked what kind of work I was doing, and I told him lawn maintenance, landscaping. He said if I was doing physical work I shouldn't do any exercising when I got home, that I should just relax. He said I had too much tension in my upper body, and that it would be bad for my heart. He kept feeling my energy and then he pointed to my left forearm and said I had hurt that too. I thought he meant my wrist so I said, "No, I hurt this wrist," and pointed to my right wrist. I had injured it about a year earlier and it had been slow in healing. It wasn't until later that day that I remembered that very morning I'd had muscle soreness on the outside of my left forearm. Evidently he was able to detect muscle soreness I had already forgotten about, and he was able to feel it from scanning energy in my back.

After a few minutes of this evaluation he had me go over to the carpeted area of the garage. Angela said, " You do what he does," and we started going through a series of gentle exercises that took about an hour. Angela stayed at the table and read a book. After the exercising Mr. Yueng had me sit in a chair and do about forty five minutes of seated meditation with elbows down by my side, hands out in front palm down, and fingers extended. Then he started going over me again with his hands about a foot away from me. He would do this for a few minutes, then leave for a few minutes, then come back and do it some more. He seemed to be concentrating mostly on my forearms. After doing this several times he was pointing his fingers at my forearms, and my fingers started making little jerking motions and in the muscles in my forearms I felt little pops or clicks in my forearm muscles like tension or adhesions were being released. Meanwhile, back at his garage, I had now been sitting in this position for quite a while and my weak upper back muscles got tired and were starting to hurt. I was pretty sure he could detect the pain and I was thinking, "come on, give me a break." But he didn't let me off the hook, and my back started hurting a lot.

I had heard a lot of these old masters would make you do a meditation for a long time, sometimes an hour or more, and if you weren't willing to go through the pain then you weren't really cut out to be their student. So I went through the pain. When time was up, he massaged my fingers, hands, arms, shoulders, neck, and back. We then did a couple more minutes of gentle cooling down type exercises. After that he came over and looked at my chest for a second, then he put one hand on my back behind my left lung and the other hand on my chest in front of my left lung and moved his head in close like he was listening to something. He told me my lungs weren't opening all the way, then he said, "You come back next week, same time," and he took me to the back door and said good bye. So that meant I had been accepted as a student, but there had been no talk of money or payments or anything of the sort.

Later that afternoon I noted I was feeling really

good, and I thought it was because I was so re- laxed. A long time later I realized that I felt so good mainly because I had been filled with a lot of pure, healthy chi energy, but since I couldn't feel energy at the time, I didn't know it. It had a strong effect, being more relaxed and energized made me feel very good, and that made me quite cheerful, both of which were rare for me back then.

The next day I had a Tai Chi class so I told Andy about my first visit with Mr. Yueng. Andy told me: "Watch him like a hawk," and that is the best advice I have ever gotten, and probably the best advice there is for students of these arts. It is amazing, the details and "secrets" you can catch if you observe very carefully, ones that can be easily missed if you don't.

I was Mr. Yueng's first real chi kung student, and I was the motivation for him teaching. Angela would have told him that I was a good student who practiced a lot and loved learning these arts. In addition, since he had touched me at the res- taurant, he knew about our previous past life con- nections.

I continued going back to see Mr. Yueng each week for about eight years and I learned about things I had thought were impossible. Little by little I dis- covered he was not just a Chi Kung master but that he was a powerful wizard and a Taoist immortal.

8 - PRACTICING THE
PATH OF POWER

I continued going back to see Mr. Yueng each week and it was the same thing each time. He had a two story house, and the back third of the lower floor was like a three car garage, consisting of a big open room going all the way across the back, with two garage doors. Since we exercised in his garage I would drive up the alley, park behind the house, and enter through the garage door at the back. The garage door was one of those big old metal units that rolled up towards the ceiling, and it made a huge racket whenever he opened or closed it so it was not possible to enter unknown to the neighbors. This space in the basement was our practice room. It had the two garage doors, one in the middle section and one which was on the left if you were looking at it from outside. I would knock, Mr. Yueng would raise the noisy thing, and we said hello to each other. After closing the door we'd took position and start doing our practice. There was nothing formal about it. There was no bowing or calling him master. It was all very casual, and I was told later that he did not like being called master, he just wanted to be called by his first name, which was Fook, but I couldn't bring myself to be so familiar with him so out of respect, I always called him Mr. Yueng, which Andy also did, and most other people who knew him did.

He had carpeting on the floor, so I took my shoes off but we usually left socks on, it depended on the weather. Even though he had been living in the States for several decades he spoke very little English so we didn't talk much before class.

The garage bay to my left was separated from the other two bays by a waist high wall that went back two thirds of the way, with fabric hanging from above. making this area semi concealed, making it not visible when the light on that side was off. He used that space for storage, and for an altar. The altar was a tall open shelf, which reached to above head height. It had brass metal legs and frames, and glass shelves. Across from it, up against the low wall was a type of high chair which also had a high foot rest. Once I sat in that high chair facing his little altar when he was in the other room. When he came into the garage and saw me, he gave me a stern look and with a quick jerk of his head to the side he motioned for me to get off his chair in a hurry, which I did. It seemed he didn't want me messing up his meditation spot with my relatively uncultivated and dirty energy.

The central shelf of the altar had a framed picture of a person wearing orange robes, which I think are Buddhist. He said this was his teacher, however he said our Chi Kung was purely Taoist, untouched by Buddhism in any way. There was an incense-burner there, along with some small bowls with fruit in them. In the central position was a bright red statue of some raggedy looking old man. Mr. Yueng told me this was a statue of a famous beggar saint someone had given to him. I assumed he was honoring it in the central position because it was a nice gift. It wasn't until decades later that Steve Smith, Mr. Yueng's designated inheritor, told me Mr. Yueng was a member of a secret society called the Beggar Hands sect, or the Beggar Clan. Steve said we were also in it via family lineage. It turns out that the family lineage we are in isn't only the physical one. It includes generations of spirits which reincarnate and teach each other each generation.

This group has been so well concealed throughout history that until recently, the public assumed it was nothing more than an ancient fictitious myth. Anyway, I thought that was special, being a member of a humble group of warriors so secret, that people assumed it to be mythical.

I met one guy who'd been in Hong Kong and met a mysterious old Chi Kung master that he'd dreamed about a couple of times before meeting him. This master had been in the Red Boat Opera and was also in the Beggar Hands Clan. He practiced some Nei Kung with the guy a few times and it was so physical it was brutal. This sounds so much like my Tien Shan Chi Kung that I'm betting it was. It is my theory that the Beggar Clan were the assassins, and they were working inside the opera.

With Mr. Yueng there was never any talking during the practice, neither during the standing moving part, nor during the sitting exercises and meditation. He didn't say a word, and that was fine with me since I had learned how to carefully observe and imitate movement with my Tai Chi. Tai Chi does require a lot of verbal explanation, but for the Nei Kung path of power the only possible way to really learn it is via silent observation and imitation. There are many reasons why real Nei Kung, those vast systems of practice that are designed to produce powerful masters, is taught silently and I won't get into them here, but Lao Tzu, who was a high level Chi Kung master, wrote about it. When he wrote, *"those who speak don't know and those who know don't speak,"* he wasn't just referring to Taoist masters in general as much as he was referring to Chi Kung teachers, because Tai Chi is best learned with verbal instruction and feedback. Lao Tzu also wrote a parallel sentiment: *"the sage teaches without speaking."* You may wonder how a sage, a storehouse of wisdom, can teach something if he doesn't say anything? Well I found out exactly how that works when I was a student of Mr. Yueng. One of the many reasons for it is that spirituality is silent, and meditation only does its work silently.

During our practices we would stand in the central bay of the three section garage, with him near the house end and the door into the hallway while I stood back in the middle of the garage door end. I never stopped to think about how cool it was for me to be the only student of a powerful Taoist wizard, because I didn't know he was powerful or a wizard. I knew he was the most advanced master I would ever meet and so I just did whatever he wanted me to as well as I could. What I thought was cool was that I was learning from a Chi Kung master who was the top Kung Fu master on the West Coast, and Bruce Lee's main kung fu teacher, effectively making me Bruce's kung fu brother. I didn't know just how special the Chi Kung was for quite a long time. It's not my nature to think such things. I just accepted it as part of the natural flow of my life that I had fallen in to.

I was the only one practicing with Mr. Yueng for a month, and then Angela joined us for our afternoon practices, She was staying there at Mr. Yueng's house, and working at the University of Washington hospital. She changed her work shift so she could be there in the afternoons and act as translator for us.

After a few months of this we were going through our usual routine and were in a position where we were bending over to the side with our arms out behind us when the word "chink" popped into my head - silently - but it wasn't so quiet in my head, it was more like a yell, a psychic yell. Right then, Mr. Yueng lost his balance and had to wave his arms to regain it, he then continued with the exercise. It was obvious to me he had heard my little comment, and I was absolutely mortified. I didn't know where that word came from or why it popped into my head all of a sudden, because the word hadn't entered my mind before that, nor had any other derogatory term.

I'm not racist, and I had the utmost respect for Mr. Yueng, but I did have racist parents, and I came from a family of five boys who were nothing if not permanently engaged in the sport of insulting and calling each other names much. I think what it came from though, was my propensity to make unkind comments to myself, in my head, about some of the different people I saw that struck me as weird, different, unfriendly or unkind and this propensity was already being healed although I didn't know it at the time. All I knew was that it was very upsetting, and it continued to be upsetting to me when it started happening over and over again in following classes. Now I knew he could hear me when that word popped into my head, and it hurt each time it happened. I couldn't make it stop, and it would flash into my mind usually two or three times during a class. I also now knew that he was psychic enough to know of the torment it was putting me through. I tried hard to control my thoughts and have it not appear in my mind, but I didn't have that much skill yet. It started bothering me to the point where I actually dreaded going to class, and I did skip one or two. Then one time after this had been going on for a couple of months, I told him, while we were sitting together at the table that I had a problem.

His answer was unexpected. He said that he knew about it and to not worry because the same thing had happened to him when he started Chi Kung. That was that. No other discussion. It offered no solution of the kind you might expect from one of the "talking teachers," but it showed acceptance, understanding, and the promise it would end, like it did for him. It did stop right after that, probably because I was no longer masochistically torturing myself about how it was bothering him so much. This is the kind of emotional healing which often results from a high power meditation practice, and the kind of support you get from the teacher when you are on the spiritual path of the warrior. No babysitting. No excuses. You fix your own mess … or you don't … on your own.

After a couple of month,s another guy, Larry, started coming to class, so it was, Larry, myself, and Angela in class now. When Larry started coming to classes, we started a new tradition, which was sitting around the little round table before and after class and talking about stuff. Mr. Yueng said we could ask anything we wanted to, and said there would be no secrets. What an amazing opportunity, don't you think? It is quite common for teachers to keep some secrets from their students, so to have a master say no secrets and really mean it is very rare. However we weren't very good at asking questions nor did we know enough about Chi Kung yet to ask the right questions anyway!

He often cooked rice on his little kitchen stove while we students were doing our hour long sitting meditation and it smelled fantastic, like good buttered popcorn only better. I asked him how he cooked the rice to make it smell so good and he said that was a secret. So a secret or two remained, it seemed ... which I thought was quite funny.

Once, I broke a bone in my foot, but it was just a little sliver of bone. I had been running down a slope in a park with my wolf/malamute dog and stumbled. The ligament going down the side of my leg got stretched too much and tore off a little piece of bone where it was anchored to the side of the heel bone. Later that night it was getting real swollen and my whole foot started turning purple and black. I called up Mr. Yueng about ten o'clock at night and told him I had hurt my foot. He said to come over so I drove to his house in South Central Seattle. When I got there he had me sit in a chair and put my foot up on his leg as he sat in a chair in front of me. He did some energy projection on it and then raised my foot up and squeezed out all the swelling, which hurt quite a bit. I guess he pushed the swelling down my leg, but it just went away. Then he produced a small bottle of black liquid that smelled like it had some alcohol in it. He rubbed that black liquid on my foot and ankle, then wrapped a cloth on it which he soaked in the black liquid. It was then bound up tightly in an Ace type stretch bandage. I was able to limp around okay, but I was pretty sure there was a broken bone, so the next morning I went to the emergency room at the University of Washington hospital to get it checked. When the doctor unwrapped the foot we saw that there was no swelling and absolutely no black and blue, which are big indicators of a broken bone. So the doctor started moving my foot from one side to the other and around, saying, does it hurt now? Does it hurt now? He moved it one way and there was a sharp pain, and then we found that I couldn't move my foot in one direction, so they took an X-ray and discovered the little sliver of bone that had been ripped off the side of my heel. The thing is that the bone had already started to heal and if I had just left it alone and wrapped, it would have been fine, but now the doctor re-broke it, so we made an appointment to see a surgeon who would reattach it with the aid of some screws.

That next week, Angela told me to not go to the surgeon because she knew of people who'd had bones connected with screws, it made them weaker. They would often break again in the same area, she said. I trusted her, because she worked in the same hospital. Accordingly I canceled my appointment for surgery and the bone healed fine by itself. It just sticks out a bit because the bone healed after it had been moved and there was a gap between the pieces.

The black liquid that Mr. Yueng put on my foot was miraculous. I had bought similar stuff, called Dit Da Jow, from a Chinese herbal store and it was the same deep black color but it was more like a paste. The stuff from the store hardly had any effect on making the black and blue from bruises go away, but the black liquid Mr. Yueng had used absolutely made all the bruising go away, to the etent there was almost no trace of it after ten hours.

I started thinking that the Dit Da Jow he made was so effective that we could market it and make a million bucks, but he said no it's another secret. He said it was a family secret, and his family would be the Red Boat Opera Company, or whatever is left of it. So he intended to teach us Chi Kung with no secrets, but wouldn't share any secrets about how to cook rice or make medicine.

In the beginning, I wasn't able to feel energy, but my Tai Chi teacher, Andy, had often talked about it as something he could feel, which made it a big mystery to me. After a couple of months of doing Chi Kung with Mr. Yueng I started to notice my pulse throbbing in my hands when I held them out with the fingers straight, but this was different. Actually I was feeling energy, but I didn't know it then. With each beat of my heart, my hands would pulse with a bit of a vibratory feeling and a feeling of fullness. It's not that my hands were vibrating, it was a rather fine high frequency vibration in the nerves of my hands. I just wrote it off as starting to be aware of the pulse in my hands. About that time, Mr. Yueng told me my energy would start alternating back and forth between one hand and the other, and sure enough, right after that when I held my hands out and focused on them the pulse alternated back and forth with each heartbeat. One beat and the right hand would pulse, the next beat the left hand would pulse. This is when I realized that the vibration I was feeling was actually the energy, and it was coinciding with my pulse. Later, little by little, when I focussed on my hands the pulsing had gone and the feeling of energy remained constant. After that I became able to feel the energy from one hand with the other hand. Mr. Yueng showed me a technique to use to project energy from my hand, and I was able to use this a couple of times on some people, and they were able to feel the energy. I felt it was a big step for me when other people could feel the energy from my hands. Making progress.

We did talk some about chi, and played a few energy games that mostly had to do with ability to sense the energy of different things while scanning above them with our hands. We also heard stories about the feats of different monks and historical figures in Taoism, along with a few of his own personal ghost stories. Sometimes we would talk for more than an hour both before and after class, which made the class take up most of the afternoon. That was fine with me because I was self employed and on a loose schedule.

Mr. Yueng's house was in South Central Seattle, a little south of the International District, and my house was in North Seattle. Mine was a small two bedroom house in the inner suburbs and it had a garage in the back. The garage had my metal fabricating shop on one side and an exercise/practice room on the other side At the time I was married to my third wife, and she had adopted a little girl from Bulgaria.

After I had acquired the rudimentary ability to feel and project chi from my hands, I was in my garage on the side which my wife had fixed up nicely for her belly dance group to practice in and drink wine. I was sitting on the floor cross legged, and holding a big imaginary ball about five feet in diameter in front of me, when my six year old daughter came into the room, walked over, and stood right in front of me between my hands.   When she got there I moved my hands softly towards each other as if gently compressing a big five foot balloon, and she started shaking and shuddering violently. When I saw this I stopped pressing on the "energy ball," and she stopped shuddering. I guess that got her energy circuits switched on in a hurry! Right after that Mr. Yueng told us we were not to do any energy work on children five or under because it would fry their circuits, so that was close. Until then I'd had no idea that pressing softly on an imaginary ball with my hands each two feet from a person, constituted energy work.

Much of what we were learning was to use our hands like sensing antennas. This was important all throughout the practice from the beginning levels to end. We practiced feeling rocks and crystals that were sitting on a wood table by passing our hands over them back and forth slowly, palm down about six inches above them. The reason for the slow-moving scanning motion is it makes it easier to notice the difference in the energy as you go from one to the next and also to locate the position of the crystal by feeling its location rather than looking. I call this ability Radar Hands and it can get rather acute, both in the sending and in the sensing. Some people, like Angela, could hold an object made in Egypt centuries ago, in her hands for a few seconds, and then talk about the character and emotions of the person who made it so long ago.

As I played around with this, I discovered as I walked, that I could feel the difference between different surface i was walking over. For example when walking from soft grass to a hard concrete sidewalk I could feel the change by holding my hands palm down waist high and just walking steadily. This is something which is done in Bagua Chi Kung but they do it while walking in circles. When I do this kind of "circle walking" inside a room, then I'm able to feel my hands passing through the energy-field of the Earth. If I focus on it, I can feel my head moving through the energy field of the Earth. For a while I did a lot of Chi Kung in my back yard with my back to a big cedar tree, and I got so I could feel the location of the tree with my back as I rolled from one side to the other without touching it.

I was doing a lot of backpacking then, going deep into the wilderness in the incredible Cascade Mountains of Washington state, for five or six days at a time. On these trips I would often aim my hand out to the side as I passed trees along the trail. At first I could feel trees going by a foot away from my hand, but with some months or years of occasional practice, I got so I could feel some bigger trees that were twelve feet away as I went by. Sometimes in the city park I would aim my hands at a tree, walk towards it, and see how far away I could begin to sense the energy of it. Once I tried this on a big old giant sequoia tree standing in the sun in Seaward Park in Seattle, and I felt the energy strongly by twenty feet away. I thought that was so amazing I told Mr. Yueng about it. He and Angela both came with me to check it out. It wasn't so far from his house. A young student of mine came with us, and when we got to the tree Mr. Yueng put one hand on the young man's back and the other on the tree. He said he was transferring the sick energy from the student to the tree. He also said giant sequoias are best for healing nerves and brains. Tree Chi Kung is an extensive yet little known science, which is best for getting rid of sick energy. Everyone, except for one in a million, like Mr. Yueng, has what we call sick energy, and you can feel it when you become very sensitive to energy. The basic way that Tree Chi Kung is done is to stand in a meditation posture called "embracing the tree", which is the same as "holding the ball." Holding the ball with your arms around the tree but without touching it. Touching, physical contact, masks the feeling of energy that you can feel on your skin. Another good way to do Tree Chi Kung is by using Bagua Chi Kung circle walking methods, but do it will going around a tree and focussing on the tree.

I used to do tree standing meditation in the 'Embrace the tree' or "holding the ball" posture. It was like hugging the tree but without physical touching, just doing a meditation/energy exchange. Another thing I practiced while in the mountains was checking campsites for recent use. The Washington mountains are the steepest in the world and level spots to put tents on are few and far between, which is why I always used a hammock or a bivy bag. Since the campsites were so rare and so obvious, when I got to one I would scan the energy at the site with my hand about waist high, palm down, and see I could feel if the tent site had been recently occupied. It got so I could tell if one or two people had been in the tent, and which way their heads and feet were oriented. If there was more than one tent spot in a camp I could feel which ones had been used. How many days prior I didn't know, but I assume it was the previous evening that people slept in those spots.

The people's energy I felt in these remote high altitude camp sites was always strong and vibrant and nice feeling. their energy blended so well with mine that I didn't notice any difference in my body, I only felt with my hands. Once though, I tried scanning the energy at a tenting platform in a car camping ground in Northern Montana near Glacier National Park, and it made me feel sick. That way it was possible to know the person who had slept in that spot was feeling bad physically, they were no doubt sick or sickly, whereas backpackers that spend days doing many miles of altitude gain going back into the high mountain wilderness are full of vitality and vibrant healthy energy. This lesson at the car cam ground taught me you sense how other's feel inside your own body, which is true hysical empathy. It is how diagnostic work for Chi Kung healing methods is done.

I used to go hiking in the Washington mountains frequently when I was in my forties and fifties. I joined the "Northwest Hikers" online forum and made some acquaintances to go hiking with. Most of them were younger, and some of the ones in better aerobic condition were able to keep up with me on my way up into the mountains. On the way down I was a little slower because going down is hard on the knees. A younger guy I often went camping deep into the wilderness with, was Dave Rocky. He was a strong hiker and didn't mind going into the rough areas with difficult trails or no trails. Because the mountains are so steep, you can't just go anywhere you want, like you can on most of the mountains around here, because a lot of the ways "cliff out." There are definite trails you need to use to get past the many impassable areas, but there are also millions of acres up above most of the trees, where you can get off the trail and go exploring all over the mountain. This is what we would do in the days following setting up our high camp. It was so beautiful, it was like being in an enchanted land. You could say Dave was a bit crazy, or a bit impractical when it came to hiking safety, and I wonder if he's still alive now. He had some bad falls while solo hiking. He didn't break any bones but he got some hellacious giant swollen bruised areas on his thighs, butt, and arms; and had some difficulty walking for awhile. We'd

Steve Gray

be wandering up some remote valley looking for some long lost trail to get up some thousand feet of nearly vertical rock wall and he would point up some ravine and say: "Hey let's go up that way," then he would add: "this part looks doable."

Well, that part which looked doable was only the lower *ten percent* of the way to the high snowy basin up above, and oftentimes the part you couldn't see would get very 'interesting'. Being such an easy going pushover kind of guy, I agreed to go along.

On his insistence there were three of us. We went up the steep wash littered with gravel and boulders, because everywhere else was a nearly vertical cliff. We went up the part that looked do-able, and it was doable. Higher up, the wash be-came steeper; a sand, dirt, and gravel slope where you couldn't get any more traction to go upwards. Each attempted step upwards resulted in a slide back down, accompanied by a little landslide of dirt and gravel onto the person below. We should have turned around then, but no. The good news, we thought! was that part of the cliff area wasn't so smooth. It was what you might call a bumpy cliff, consisting of a lot of fractured rock which offered a lot of handholds.

So, since Davey boy could go no further up the loose wash, he went over to the rock area, with me following, and the third guy pretty far back down there. At first there were some narrow ledges here and there which we scrambled up using hands and feet, but those generally went away, and we graduated to hand and foot climbing up the rocks. It wasn't so bad because there were enough handholds. At that point, looking downwards wasn't so much fun, because the valley floor, chock full of big granite boulders, was waaay down there. What we didn't know, was that the rock face we were on got just a wee bit steeper as it went further up. It got to the point where you think, "shit, should I go back down, should I have gone back down?" But by then it's too late, you can't go back down. It's too steep and you can't lean out from the rock face far enough in order to see where the lower footsteps are. Of course we had no ropes or rock-climbing gear, Dave and the other guy had left that stuff back at the camp, and I had no intention of using ropes or rock climbing gear myself. Even if we had tied up with a rope it would have been no good because if one guy slipped and fell off he would just pull the other two down with him. That left two choices. The first is you continue going up even though it's getting steeper and the handholds are getting smaller and more difficult. The other choice is you wait there on the cliff until a rescue team comes to get you, which would be three or four days since your friend would require a couple of days to hurry back to the highway to get assistance ... and it freezes at night! So we continued!

117

At the top of the giant cliff face was a beautiful little basin, with a very cold little lagoon in a small rocky plain surrounded by tall dark majestic peaks full of snow and sheer blackish rock faces. We were way above the tree line. We found the correct trail for the way down, into the valley and back to our high camp. It was a fairly easy trail really, completely safe compared to the way up!

I've been on cliffhangers like that before, when I was a young teenager in Venezuela, stuck on a little dirt cliff above a dark ravine in the jungle outside of Caracas. Actually it wasn't so high and a controlled fall/slide down into the ravine probably wouldn't have resulted in injuries. On that occasion the guy that I was with continued and went home. He left me there, all alone on the side of some cliff in the jungle in the middle of nowhere. Finally I forged on and made it out of the ravine and into the tangle of brush up above. We had gone into that ravine because it had little to none of the tangle of vegetation that was up above, and so the going was actually a lot easier, and it was cool. A very cool place to explore, and with a noticeably cooler temperature than the hot cloudless baking savannah/jungle cover of the northern mountain ranges that border the Southern Caribe Sea. The big modern city of Caracas we lived in then was in the middle of that mountain range where it was still very hot but noticeably cooler than the coast. It was about an hour and a half drive from Caracas down to the coast where we used to go to the beaches. We kids would spend most of our time snorkeling out in the coral reefs, exploring and looking at all the colorful coral and fish. I never tried scuba diving with an oxygen tank because all the brightest colors are closest to the surface. It's more of a fun challenge to take a big breath and dive down to and around some interesting fish or rock formation. To dive down to pick up something off the sandy floor to prove you got there, and then blow hard like a whale when surfacing to get the water out of the snorkel, was where it's at for the kids.

I love snorkeling and swimming underwater with fins on, swimming like a dolphin swims, loving it because it's like having the three dimensional freedom to fly around in space that I've had in my dreams. Wanting to fly, that has always been me, and flying underwater got me close.

There's obviously the problem with limited breath though, so in the many pools we had when I was a kid, I learned to hyperventilate and then swim so softly and gently, like in a slow motion trance, that I used as little energy as possible for swimming and had more oxygen left to drift silently underwater. It got so I could go back and forth up to three pool lengths on one breath, and that was in pretty big swimming pools. Other times I'd stay more or less in one area of the pool pushing off with my feet from first one wall and then off the next wall or the bottom, doing under-water aerobatics along the way. It was swimming the way I was later flying in my flying dreams, and loving it!

So what does all this have to do with the Taoist Path of Power? Well I'll tell you, the path of power is just naturally made for those who have an ad-venturous and somewhat daring spirit, someone who has had a good scare or two under their belts, because there are more of those to come, and it can be dangerous too, in several ways. It's for people who like nature and makes you want to become a hermit so you can get away from it all, to a pure place where you can live in peace … surrounded by nice clean natural energy. It made me want to do that, and I finally succumbed to it when I moved to the high mountains of Southern Ecuador.

I went fasting one time in the mountains of Wash-ington in the drier Eastern side of the Cascades. I went hiking up along the big Entiat River, which went up the long Entiat Valley, and into the en-chanting high altitude Entiat Basin wilderness, which still had plenty of big snow banks even in late July. Along the way there were different routes you could use to climb up, into, and along the Entiat Range. You could go via the valley floor or you could go up on either side and along the ridge tops. I had decided to do a four day backpack there while juice fasting because it was away from food and that would cure the temptation problem. Juice fasting, is where you take a little sip of very diluted fruit juice whenever you feel a hunger pang. This little tiny boost of sugar makes the hunger go away for awhile but it's basically just water, so your digestive system is not activated. I brought two small pop bottles with frozen juice concentrate. One was orange juice, and the other was frozen blueberry juice. When I got to my base camp I put the bottles in an ice cold stream. What a gorgeous place that was, with thick stands of close growing fir trees interspersed with bright green grassy fields, and very high sheer rock walls going far above on all sides. From my camp I could see a thin misty waterfall drifting down through space along the side of the cliff nearest to my hammock. It refracted the sun with a bright patch of rainbow color which descended through the waterfall as the sun rose.

I had brought my three legged stool along on that trip. From Venezuela, it had strong bamboo legs and a leather seat top which came off and allowed folding. I was at low enough altitude to permit fires so I started a small fire in the little clearing where I was sitting on the low stool. Out of the blue I started making a pulling motion, reaching down and pulling upwards with a bird's beak grasping motion. After doing that for a few minutes I scanned the spot by moving my hand slowly back and forth over it, and found I could feel a flow of energy there like a little fountain, which was pretty neat. So I made the pulling lifting motion some more in that spot, tested it, noticed it got stronger, and then forgot about it and went to bed in my hammock.

The next two nights I spent up at the end of the valley, in the high altitude Entiat Basin with its many glacial moraines and big slopes strewn with rocks, gravel, and boulders. Up there the flat spots were rare and the trees were too small to use a hammock, so I slept in my bivy bag.

It took a day to get up to high camp with enough extra time in the afternoon to set up camp, and go exploring a bit. From there I spent the first day going up onto the head of the stark and rocky Entiat Range, far above the tree line. Often in this part of the world the steep sided mountains are topped with some steep gravel and rock slopes that permit unlimited wandering in most directions - until you get to a spot where it cliffs out and you have to find a different route or go back. After the second night there I spent the following day exploring and wandering around the gravel and snow slopes at the end of the snowy, rocky, valley. Then I packed up camp and hiked down to the same place where I had my original base camp to spend the final night. I had another small fire and set my stool up in the same place it had been before. After sitting at the fire for a while I remembered what I had done with pulling on the energy from the ground, so I swept my hand back and forth over the spot to check it. I was able to feel that little fountain of energy, it was still flowing up out of the ground, which it must have been doing continuously for three days. You can feel which way energy is flowing with your hand mainly by which side, palm or back of hand, that you feel it on most, and then by turning your hand over to check to see how it feels on the other side. To me it often feels like a gentle or sparkly breeze.

Now this is important to note. That little fountain of energy flowing out of the ground breaks the laws of physics, which I know very well. The laws of physics clearly state that energy will not flow by itself, it always has to have some force, a source of higher pressure, hotter, if you will, in order to project it outwards into a cooler environment. Making energy flow requires some kind of constant power source to push it along, and yet here in the mountains the same little stream of energy was flowing all by itself for at least three days.

That's kind of amazing, I call it 'seeing the mystery,' which the ancient sage, Lao Tzu, wrote about in chapter one of The Tao Te Ching, and I love seeing the mystery. He wrote that those who are desireless can see the mystery. Seeing the mystery (some would call it magic) is something that happens more and more as you progress in real Nei Kung and it is highly entertaining.

I have read that evolution will take full advantage of all quantum effects, which strikes me as a fundamental truth, so it seems probable this sensing of energy is the body's extreme fine-tuning allowing it to tap into those quantum effects. Either that, or the 'laws' of physics are simply incorrect. Some people might say it's magic, and a master once told me that if you practice one of the authentic Taoist lineages that you *will* experience magic. I just feel that using the word magic doesn't explain anything useful, so why bother. I prefer to call it seeing the mystery. This ability to make energy flow with your hand is not so hard to learn, and most of my newer students are able to feel energy and make it flow flow after practicing for a few months.

I discovered the spot where I always stood in my garage to do Chi Kung was energized from floor to ceiling with a beam of energy flowing upwards, and I suppose it continues up through the ceiling and roof. I found when I went away to Hawaii for vacation that when I returned and tested the spot after being gone for three weeks that the energy flow was still there and pretty strong.

The spot where I stand in the practice room here in Ecuador to do chi kung now is highly energized but I haven't been away from here for much time to be able to test how long it might remain flowing in my absence. Once a student who was quite sensitive to energy came here for a couple of weeks and instinctively found the location of my practice spot when he first entered the practice room. He went over, and stood in the energy beam. He said the energy there felt wonderful, and he got a bit giddy.

Energizing places or things was a new and wondrous world I had entered. Mr. Yueng used to leave trails of energy behind as he walked through the garage, and if you were sensitive enough you could feel those trails and follow them. What a marvelous thing this path of the wizard was turning out to be, and it kept me, with my scientific inquiring mind, very interested and curious.

Mr. Yueng had so much energy, and my Tai Chi teacher, Andy, is so sensitive to energy, that once when Andy was walking along a sidewalk in downtown Seattle and Mr. Yueng was inside a big building, Andy felt his energy and was able to follow it in order to locate him.

During this time when I was learning to sense energy with my hands, I was also learning to project energy from my hands, and I played a few games with my students to check this out. Early on, they were able to feel energy from my palm if I shone it on their hands from a foot or two away. Later we checked to see if they could feel the change in energy on their faces when I alternated between aiming my palm at their face and turning it away.

A couple of them were able to feel it up to fifteen feet away. I'm so glad that Mr. Yueng allowed me to teach from early on, because I learned so much from my students, and it kept me practicing all the time.

One of the thousands of exercises we learned was to energize a section of wall in front of us and at the same time see if we can feel it. This has two aspects. One is that the wall itself is becoming energized so you can feel that. Additionally, your energy is reflecting off the wall and back to your hands, so you can feel that too. A harder and denser wall, like rock or concrete, can be energized more strongly, and it stays energized and re-radiates energy outwards for a longer period of time than a wood wall can. A harder surface also reflects energy better, so, as I said earlier, there are two parts to it although they feel the same. At first you can feel your energy reflecting off the wall and then as it slowly becomes more and more energized you feel that additional energy added to the reflected energy.

This was done as a moving exercise, so we would be moving around, and see how far away from the wall we could get and still feel it. When you get far enough away from the wall or object, the feeling gets confused with the feeling of the background energy field of the Earth. I know I can feel the local energy field because when I focus on it I can feel myself moving through it with my hands or my head if I walk smoothly in a meditational manner. I learned this ability because I practiced this kind of sensitivity exercise with my hands, and the reason I can also feel it in my head is because I really like head energy and have focussed a lot of high power meditations on sending my energy, which got ever stronger, up to my head.

We also did some meditations which were a combination of "third eye focu," combined with different subtle movements of the head ... or hands ... but mostly the head. These kinds of exercises, if you focus on them enough, lend you the ability to perceive the energy of other people and their location in a certain sphere that extends outwards from your body. You could think of this sphere as your aura, which can grow big indeed if you follow the Taoist path of power, and the volume of this sphere of knowing of the presence of other people or animals can become very large for a hermit who spends much of his time meditating alone on some mountain. For example, there are stories of hermits who can sense someone approaching from miles away, and some warriors can sense when a person is near, and where they are.

I was able to use this method to feel the location of the big cedar tree in my back yard, with my head, neck, or back, when I did Chi Kung with my back facing it. This kind of sensitivity is useful in self defense and safety in general, and is something that has been with us from prehistoric, more instinctive times. For example, once I was doing a little Bagua circle walking around the big cedar tree in my back yard. I walked around it with both palms aimed at the tree to both feel the energy of the tree and locate myself the correct distance from it with eyes closed. As I came around I felt the energy of one low branch as it neared my forehead and so I ducked automatically, without thinking. If I had been thinking I would have known the branch isn't low enough to hit my head, but it's close. My ducking was just flinching instinctively in response to a proximity threat. Later I was practicing with one of my students while we were at a semi-secret martial arts training camp in the mountains of Northeastern Oregon. I was blindfolded, and he was swinging a wood sword at me, admittedly quite slowly, and I was able to sense where the sword strike was going to go as if seeing a line in the air with eyes closed, andIi was able to move to get out of way of this line. This was moreso a type of psychic reading of mind rather than energy reading of body or object. I think it worked because he was focussing a lot on the sword strike motion that time, because later when we did it, he tried to hide his intent ... and then I did poorly in knowing where the sword cut was headed.

With this kind of sensitivity to both psychic and body activity of another, it is possible to feel the intent and decision the moment a person decides to attack, and you can also feel the strong nerve impulse and muscle tension of a beginning strike. It's almost like you know when someone is going to attack you the same moment they do,. Accordingly you can respond appropriately, with plenty of time.

I started seeing people's auras. At first I could only see it around Andy when we were out in the park and he was lecturing us about some aspect of Tai Chi. When I was sitting down and he was standing up with the whitish colored sky behind him, his aura showed up quite well as a lighter band radiating out six to nine inches around his head and torso. Since Andy had more energy than your average person it was an easier way to start. Later I was able to see auras of other people, like my students, or people in a theater, as long as they had a smooth light-colored wall behind them. The coolest one happened in Chi Kung class. His garage being in his basement, Mr. Yueng had put very dark shades over the small windows, and he would make it very dark when we were doing the sitting meditation, nearly pitch black. Once, during the meditation, I opened my eyes and peeked at the guy sitting across from me. He had a bright white light shining out from his whole body for about a foot. It wasn't like a faintly brighter area around someone that I had seen during the daytime. I was seeing someone glowing in the dark!

After that, I made a new tongue-in-cheek definition for our practice. Our goal is to cultivate enough energy so that we glow in the dark.

After that I sort of lost interest in seeing auras. I stopped practicing it, and the ability dwindled. I have found that many times I'll experience some psychic ability and think to myself, "that was cool," and then lose interest in further developing it. I have found that this tendency is likened to the Taoist concept of not getting sidetracked into detours. Many of my students also developed the ability to see auras.

Mr. Yueng told us that Tien Shan Chi Kung is a purely Taoist system, that had not been stained by Buddhism in any way. Whilst learning this amazing practice, I also started learning more about its source. I discovered that Taoism is a warrior tradition. Many of its saints and gods were warriors. It was common back in those dangerous lawless times, because everyone practiced self defense as if their lives depended on it, for entirely practical reasons.

Of course, anyone who is a warrior, naturally wants to be powerful. Who ever heard of anyone wanting to be a wimpy warrior? It doesn't happen. Unlike some of the New Age types who seem to disdain power, Taoists have a healthy attitude towards power, realizing that it is simply a way to get things done more effectively, and that the best way to become powerful is to be virtuous. This then makes the pursuit of power align with spiritual goals and we find that real Nei Kung, the path of chi power, is also the spiritual path of the warrior, and at higher levels this same path becomes the spiritual path of the wizard, because a wizard is an advanced and powerful warrior. Taoism is a warrior tradition, and that is embodied most in the way so many of the practices are so closely linked to self defense. In fact, real Nei Kung, the Taoist path of the wizard, is an official part of the Taoist religion. Official, yes, and although official it is often so far underground that almost no one can find it.

As you probably know by now, the path of the warrior is not necessarily about fighting ... at least not fighting physically.

9 - ENLIGHTENMENT EXPERIENCE

Around a half year after starting to learn Tien Shan Chi Kung the four of us, Mr. Yueng, Angela, Larry, and I, were sitting around the little table in his garage before class when Mr. Yueng brought up the subject of enlightenment. He told us he thought it would take five years for us to have our enlightenment experience. The next week we were once again sitting around the table and he said there were so many distractions in modern life that it would take ten years instead of five. Well it turned out he was right the first time ... it took only five years.

It happened when I was forty six or forty seven. The first thing that happened was I came to class, and after going in through the garage door Mr. Yueng took me over to the back wall and showed me somethin. He had an arrangement of three of the most beautiful silk roses sitting there in a little vase. They looked so realistic partly because they had drops of resin on the leaves and rose petals, looking like droplets of water. There was a red one, a pink one, and a white one. He said, "Pick one for yourself," so I picked the red rose. Then he said, "Pick one for your wife," so I picked the white one. Lastly he said, "Pick one for your daughter," so I took the pink one. That was all the roses. I didn't stop to wonder why would he give me a gift like that? Why did he give the gift to me and not to Larry? I didn't think about it and I didn't care. I did take the flowers home and put them in a nice flower vase in the living room.

It wasn't till a couple of days later that I found out what the gift was all about, although I didn't make the connection till a few days after that. Mr. Yueng was just showing me that he already knew what was going to happen by giving me the present before the fact.

I was at home, on the computer, on the old internet. I had joined the AOL forums, which was the first internet forum for the general public, which had instant messenger. I had joined the Buddhism and Taoism message boards on AOL in order to learn, make acquaintances, and have some fun at the expense of the fundamentalists. There are fundamentalists everywhere, including in some sects of Buddhism. I had made online friends via the Buddhism forum with a lady from India named Radhika, who was temporarily living in New Jersey. She was a close disciple of Sai Baba and a wonderful person, and since both she and I have green eyes I used to call her my green eyed sister. At the time, I was playing the drug manufacturer's favorite game, which was taking some medicine that had terrible side-effects, in order to cure something that they had given to me with a previous medicine. I could tell Radhika had a pure heart. She was very helpful and even offered to fly from New Jersey to Seattle to help take care of me. I declined her offer as I was getting by okay and I had no idea what she could do to help this situation with the bad side effects of the medicine. I didn't know that her gift was more along the lines of spiritual healing. We continued messaging and then the conversation ran out of steam. Right at the end, she asked me a couple of rather strange questions. She said: "Do you believe in me?", and I said yes. Then she said: "Do you have faith in me?", and I said yes.

We signed out of the AOL messenger and then it happened, instantly, like snapping your fingers or flipping a light switch. I was aware of a profound change in my state of being. One second everything was 'normal', and the next second it was completely gone, like being teleported into an entirely different universe. Mental tension vanished, and thinking disappeared, to be replaced by pure awareness. When the thinking and mental tension disappeared, my sense of self disappeared also. Thinking, mental and physical tension, and sense of self are all inextricably tied together. This aspect of the experience, which is your sense of self going away, is what some religious cartoonists like to call "being one with everything," which I feel is either an exaggeration or a lie, or we can be generous here and say they are waxing poetic. (Religious Cartoonist, in this case, means people who promote different religious sects with a promise of enlightenment.)

Normal thinking and self identity were replaced by an absolute inner silence like I had never experienced before, even during deep non thinking meditation. It was deeper and more profound, and it was constant.

The other principal aspect of the enlightenment experience that is more particular to Nei Kung is that when that switch gets flipped and the experience starts there is a sudden and profound sense of bliss. Bliss is one of those words which has been overused by the New Age religious cartoonists, so it may be difficult to convey the actual feeling. Firstly, you should know that most people who use the word bliss, probably are not well acquainted with that about which they speak, because there are three kinds of bliss. The first one is physical bliss, which isn't so hard to come by with some sex or some drugs, but those are pretty limited and poor examples of how good it can actually get. The second kind of bliss, which is how I define enlightenment, is emotional bliss, and it is extremely rare. Some may confuse the state of emotional bliss with some feelings of emotional satisfaction or joy but that is not it; it is much more profound than those things. The third kind of bliss is mental bliss, which becomes possible after you master the art of non thinking. Then at times when you do think about something, that process itself can be blissful. In fact emotional bliss is the enlightenment experience. The type of emotional bliss that comes with the enlightenment experience is what you could call complete. This type of bliss comes only from the loss of identity, which itself comes from the absolute stopping of thinking. It is absolutely peaceful. It fills you with a feeling of unconditional love. This feeling of unconditional love is not directed at anything in particular. It's just a feeling you have about everything in general that is directed at anything you pay attention to, and most importantly, this feeling of unconditional love is directed at yourself.

And it lasts for three days.

So, everything is wonderful, every person and animal is wonderful, you love everything, you feel wonderful. Your mind is not cluttered with useless thoughts, so there are no worries and no problems in the world, you are in a state of complete peace.

For the record, this state is contagious. My experience started in the afternoon while I was home alone, but that night, my wife and daughter got home. She worked at a computer office job as a systems analyst for the University of Washington Hospital billing system. It was a high stress job.

The billing system would start up at midnight and if one little band-aid wasn't listed correctly, the whole system would shut down, and she would often have to get up at one or two in the morning, drive to work, and find the problem. It was much better later when she got a home terminal so she could work from home. Anyway, her job was stressful so she could be tired and grouchy, and our daughter, just back from day care, was often tired and grouchy too. It was grouchy-land and I would join in the grouching fun sometimes, but more often I would stay away from it.

This time, however, it was different, I didn't tell them anything, I would never have thought to do so unless someone asked about it. This time in the kitchen was different. This time it was a quiet and peaceful happy little get together.

The second day it was pretty much the same, except the feeling of emotional bliss was a little less, and the feeling of non identity was a little less, thinking started returning little by little and towards the end of the second day, thinking was pretty much back in the saddle, although with a notably different tone to it. It was like thoughts somehow stood out as cleaner, not stained by the chatter of the monkey mind.

The third day there was still bliss and internal quiet, but it was markedly less than the previous day, normal thinking was returning and normal life was returning with it.

As thinking returns, a person naturally wants to figure out what it is that just happened to them. Most will suspect it was enlightenment, but knowing a word definition is one thing, figuring out what it's all about is something else altogether. One of the first things you notice when thinking returns is when some profound or impossibly difficult philosophical question enters your mind, the answer to that question comes to you immediately, and you know it is the right answer! You don't think it or think that you know it, you just know it, whatever it is; it's an obvious fact - answered. This part of the experience continues for a couple of days. Some of the religious cartoonists call it Raincloud Samadhi, which is supposed to mean all the information in the universe pours into your head, all at once. Well, "all the information" is a ridiculous exaggeration. Possibly it could seem that way to some extraordinarily vociferous question-askers who like to wax poetic, but no, not all the knowledge in the universe enters into your head, although answers to specific questions do. Some Buddhist sects call these 'realizations', and the more fundamentalist the sect is the more they stress the importance of these realizations. I had some of these realizations myself, but later I forgot them and these answers faded into the distance. This was followed by the realization that those philosophical kinds of realizations are only useful for impressing others with "wisdom." However, realizations about yourself and others ... either other individuals or about human nature in general, are different. Those kinds of realizations blend together and become incorporated into your values and then your attitude, so perhaps you could say they are forgotten in a different way. They are forgotten at the superficial level of mind but remembered at the level of inner being. That is one way of portraying the Taoist attitude towards knowledge and being.

At least that's the way it worked for me, but I'm quiet and don't talk much. I'm a natural born Taoist, and Taoists appreciate the importance of not cluttering up their minds with what mostly turns out to be a lot of useless information. A person who is both very mental and a teacher of ideas, would remember the realizations and then share them with students eager to clutter up their minds with useless information. In any case, all these brilliant realizations are public now, in this age of information, you can get them for free on the internet. One big way that this kind of information has any use is to show people that there is more to the world than they might think. Mostly though, it is useful if it gets someone to begin practicing meditation.

It is a natural thing for people to do though, to focus on the mental aspect or the memory of something, and then place importance on that, rather than the experience itself.

Another aspect of a person's nature is closely tied to the enlightenment experience, and that is honesty, and most importantly self-honesty. A person must have pretty good self-honesty to even be able to have the chance for enlightenment. This is because after some time, months or years, a person ends up doing what is called "facing their dark side." Unfortunately, many people tend to be in denial, so when they get to that stage of the game, where they see their dark side, they quit meditating This means those who are left, the ones who stick with it, are not afraid to face their own worst enemy. They are warriors at heart and have an inner toughness and bravery which permits this continued exploration of the self.

The enlightenment experience ignites a process of internal alchemy, which is when real personal growth starts, and this growth is only because of a person's ruthless self-honesty. They no longer make excuses to themselves for their mistakes, and if they detect an excuse they examine their belief to see if it is true or not. Self examination, self introspection, self-honesty, that's the ticket. The self-honesty tendency was already there or they wouldn't have had the enlightenment experience, but after the experience it becomes more absolute.

That's when the problems start, because you don't just apply this ruthless honesty to yourself, you naturally apply it to everyone else as well, and savagely too. It becomes amazing to observe people being so hurtful to themselves and others, and then denying it. You wonder: how can they lie to themselves like they do? You realize they are torn up inside from internal conflict. You begin to see how so many people are so screwed up, and this realization is quite depressing. Of course you want to help them alleviate their suffering. You know this wonderful experience you had is about self-honesty and living in reality, and they badly need that. So at this point, you run the risk of becoming a kind of evangelist, wanting to share this wonderful practice you have, which made it all possible. That's what happened to me. This is what the Buddhists call being a Bodhisattva, which is where a person has their enlightenment experience and they vow to not become fully enlightened until they have assisted all others on the planet to become enlightened as well.

What happens is you try to share this marvelous thing you learned because you want to help people, not for the money. What actually happens is you discover that almost no one is interested, and of those who are interested, almost none sticks with it. So eventually you just kind of give up on that scene and say the hell with it, which is also your moment of transition from Bodhisatva to Buddha. It doesn't take long to realize people don't like evangelists.

So that's depressing too. Learning how screwed up people are is depressing, then finding out you can't help most of them is even more depressing. This is where you get to the point where plenty of people who have an enlightenment experience go on to commit suicide or go crazy … essentially weeding out the ones who aren't tough enough, weeding out the non-warriors.

So enlightenment, this thing that is so light and positive and wondrous in the beginning, inevitably becomes a dark and depressing time as the Yin Yang wheel turns from one side to the other. This difficult part is something the religious cartoonists don't tell you about. When there is a problem the warrior faces it instead of making excuses, and this problem is a big juicy one. The solution to this problem is basically giving up, not caring any more, taking the good with the bad. From your perspective you can see how people are suffering, but at other times they're so damn cute. The solution to it, really, is to just not care anymore, the mark of a Buddha they say. You can't change it so don't worry about it. I mean, you may find one or two people that you really can help go far with your practice, but you ain't never going to change the population at large.

There is also the problem of *definitions* with

enlightenment, as I've pointed out, and one of them is the way people define the post enlightenment experience. Does the enlightenment experience, combined with the realizations, add up to a higher level of enlightenment? Or does the return to more or less normal life but with some additional understandings and enhanced abilities mean that you are no longer enlightened? To answer this question we find that there is a big clue in the word itself. The word enlightened ends with the two letters "ed," and what I learned in kindergarten is if you put 'ed' at the end of a word, that means it happened in the past. Enlight-en**ed** means it's in the past, you became enlightened during your enlightenment experience, but the experience itself, the emotional bliss and non thinking, isn't there anymore, is it? It's in the past. There is not much agreement among users of those words as to what they really mean. I don't really care which way you choose. It's of no importance to me. In fact I never did care about enlightenment, either before or after it happened. However I choose to go with my own experience, and with the common word usage in that, since the word ends in 'ed', to me it is in the past. So I put it this way: I was enlightened during and shortly after my enlightenment experience, but now I'm not enlightened, just smarter. It makes more sense to me and has the added appeal of going against the percetions of the maddening crowd.

It would be nice, of course, very nice, to have this experience of emotional bliss again. I suspect if I started meditating much more, it would return. It is akin to a drug in a way, it starts and you get so high, and then it wears off and you get so low. It's the most amazing drug in the world though, you can't beat it for purity, you can't beat it for the cleanness and power.

It is truly amazing to me that everyone has within them this latent ability to experience ecstasy and profound inner silence and peace. What a marvelous thing we are, what a fantastic thing life is, to give us something like this. Yet it is almost unknown to the masses, and as such, vastly unappreciated. It truly is a mystery of the universe, how could such a thing be?

10 - MY TEACHING

While I was a student of Mr. Yueng I was fortunate to be self employed and working at home alone. Not only did this fit well with my hermit type of personality but it gave me a lot of free time to practice Chi Kung whenever the whim struck me. I had evolved from making custom wood burning stoves to solely "made to order" custom fireplace doors. The doors and the front frame retained all the high tech methods used in wood stoves in order to have a clean smoke free burn and a window that self cleans the soot off with an air wash. I ensured that my doors were better in every way than any of the competition and as a result I had mostly well-to-do customers who lived in really nice houses. The fireplace doors I made were like jewelry for their living room, their entertainment room, so heavy duty, high quality was very important to them. Some of the doors were even plated in 24K gold.

When a potential customer called me, I went to their house to measure their fireplace and explain to them the different ways an airtight fireplace door could be installed and the different styles that were available. I explained everything so they had a thorough understanding of the mechanics of the situation. Also, I was a very low key salesman. I never pushed to close a deal ... I let the customers ask me. Often I would tell them to think about it and call me if they wanted one, then leave. They appreciated it because I had just given them so much to think about and choose from, they needed some time. Truthfully, the thing which motivated me was the challenge to design and craft something exquisite. I really didn't care about the money. Many of these more well to do people really appreciated my low key attitude. Invariably, they called me back to measure their fireplace in detail, discuss the details and options, and pay the deposit.

I think this attitude of mine, to go for the art and forget the money, is a sign of potential mastery, and I know Mr. Yueng liked that about me. In fact I'll venture to say that's the kind of student that most real masters want.

After being with Mr. Yueng for about six months I got a call for a fireplace door set from a yoga teacher who taught in her basement, where she taught yoga. When I found out she was a yoga teacher I started explaining a little about Chi Kung since I was so thrilled about all the things I was experiencing. Apart from which, Chi Kung is also a kind of yoga. I started telling her about energy and Chi Kung, and she said she would like to feel some energy. At the time we were sitting cross legged on the floor looking at pictures of fireplace doors. So I had her open up her hand with palm facing up, I put my open hand about a foot above hers with my palm facing down at hers. I moved my hand a bit so she was able to feel the energy. She was kind of amazed and became curious, and then asked if I could teach her. I had no expectation of teaching anyone at that point. It simly hadn't occurred to me. So the next week when I went to see Mr. Yueng I told him about her, and Mr. Yueng said something completely unexpected: "Tell her I have a new granddaughter and welcome to the family." That was kind of a wow moment for me. Until then I hadn't thought of it being like a family, but I liked it, a lot. It gave me a wonderful sense of belonging to something, something great. Being in a Kung Fu family is taken seriously too, with your fellow students being your Kung Fu brothers and sisters, and Mr. Yueng was my Kung Fu father. His Chi Kung teacher was my grandfather. It also meant Bruce Lee was my Kung Fu brother, but only technically, because I never met him in person.

I think we had a total of three classes in the basement of that house, and there were four people. After the third class the lady called me and said the others had lost interest, so no more classes. I was later to find this was a typical reaction to this kind of exercise. In any case it got me started on the path of teaching. I put a listing in the yellow pages and made a website for it. There were a few people who came, one at a time, and so I would schedule the class time to suit their schedule.

I decided to move into a proper place of business, with a storefront on an arterial road, closer to civilization than my house in the suburbs. I figured the University area would be perfect. I encountered a lady who had just bought a rather large one story building in the University area, and fixed it up nicely. There was a big yoga room with glass walls and glass door that opened up onto an interior patio which had been made into a garden. There were also a couple of massager rooms and some nice bathrooms. I started teaching there right when the place opened for business. When I first advertised, three people came, but that quickly dwindled to two.

The owner threw a big open house one weekend and all the people who taught there came to show their stuff. There was tea and treats, and a big crowd came. I went to one of the other presentations and we sat around on the floor while the guy talked about his new-agey stuff. Afterwards we did a couple of simple visualization exercises. It was kind of pathetic actually. When it was my turn to teach, I did the usual, almost no talking and a lot of good moving Chi Kung. It was a pretty big turnout ... the room was packed with almost thirty people. After the event, the owner told me she had noticed a big difference with the visitors after my class. When people came out of the room after the other classes to have their tea and snacks, they were their usual quiet dreary selves, but when they came out after my class they were all energized, with much more body movement, talking and laughter. Maybe they themselves didn't notice the difference but the owner sure did. I thought that was neat, but not a single one of them signed up to take classes. I radiate a lot of energy when I practice and teach, and it can energize a lot of people in a fairly large room. In this case it was kind of like flushing my energy down the toilet because not one signed up. I found out later that this ability to radiate a lot of energy and energize a lot of people while practicing is something peculiar to my personal Taoist path of the wizard. Many Chi Kung masters don't acquire such abilities. They can project some energy from their hands when they want to do some healing, but they are not like non-stop fountains of healing energy which gets even stronger when they practice.

A little after that, the 'class' size at the storefront place dwindled to one, and then sometimes none. With only one person coming it didn't generate enough to pay the rent, so I stopped teaching there and started in my garage. Besides, getting ready to teach, driving for twenty minutes to someplace 'foreign', paying rent, and standing around for fifteen or twenty minutes and having no one show up gets old real fast.

I ended up teaching at home in the little garage

behind the house. One side of the garage consisted of a small room which my wife had fixed up nicely with mirrors on on side, soundproofing tile in the ceiling, and a carpet on the floor so she could host belly-dance practices with her group. It was a small room, and the building was a bit poorly made with the low ceiling sagging quite a lot towards the center. The ceiling was so low that I, being six feet two inches tall, could put my palms flat on it with my feet flat on the floor and my elbows bent a little. It was a bit low to do some of the Chi Kung movements exactly right, but I made do. The important thing was I felt much more comfortable teaching at my own home, and teaching in your garage is a time-honored tradition in the hidden arts; it's also what Mr. Yueng was doing.

Most people would come to class for a couple of weeks, or a couple of months, and then quit. Slowly I realized this system was really not for most people. I had one student who was really gung ho though, and after coming for a while wanted us to start practice at six in the morning. That was way before my normal wake up time, but I got into it, and it was a good time to practice. At one point this guy told me he was shocked I was offering this kind of stuff to the public, and later he dropped out. His friend later said he had become a bit scared. He and his friend were both professors at the University of Washington in

Seattle and knew each other. The other university professor, who was head of the department of ancient Greek and Latin literature, was my student for over ten years, until I left the north to go south of the equator. He started having more and more psychic abilities as we progressed.

I had one student who got into it because he wanted to become an energy healer. After a little more than a year, he dropped out and started doing energy healing. He was pretty good at it, but it was a mistake to quit his day job. Another one, who was my favorite student and the most enthusiastic, was a biomedical engineer and the leader of a rock and roll band. I felt worse about abandoning her when I moved to Ecuador, than I did leaving my own daughter.

There was one guy, probably in his upper thirties, that was working at Microsoft, who came for a few classes during the afternoons. He was a bit of a challenge. He was the only one in that afternoon class, and it was the third class I think, when it started happening. You see, he was kind of chubby, and that was back when being overweight wasn't the raging fashion trend that it is now. It wasn't bad, you know, but he was covered in a fair amount of pudge. During this third class I had with him, the word "fat" started popping into my head - regularly. It was annoying, and the more it went on the more annoying it got. Sometimes the word would pop into my head big and bold, like

FAT! Sometimes it would sneak in quietly around the edges of my consciousness as I was dreading the next one, like *f a t.*

However, nary a word to this effect escaped my lips, you can be sure of that. Other than that, the class was normal. At the end of class, as he was going out the door he came right up to me and said: "I'm not fat!"

Well, I was so surprised he had heard me, and so embarrassed I was speechless ... he walked out the door, never to be seen again!

He did call me the following week to let me know he was stopping coming to class because he was too busy at work, and that was credible, because Microsoft was known for having i's employees work very long hours.

About four months later he called me again and told me he had been taking some Chi Kung classes with some Chinese 'master,' and that he felt much more energy when he did Chi Kung with me than with that other guy. In short, he wanted to return as a student. I said no to his request. The reason was, I was afraid that the psychic name calling would start up again and I just didn't want to deal with it. In retrospect I realize it was a shame I chickened out, because he probably would have been a good student. Being psychic and sensitive to energy is already a good start, and he was one of the successful types who would typically do well on the spiritual path of the warrior. Another big thing is he was willing to come back in spite of having to face more psychic name calling, which shows a pretty strong determination to pursue an effective practice. If I had allowed his returned, I also could have gotten some practice keeping my psychic yap shut. I have frequently observed that people that are psychic or very sensitive to energy, are overweight. I speculated that this might be because since they have more cells in their bodies. They also have a bigger nerve network and the nerve network serves as the sensing, receiving, and sending antenna for energy in various ways, including the psychic way.

It turns out that it was actually great for me to have begun teaching so early, because I would learn new methods and variations from Mr. Yueng and then practice them with students the same week. In this way I had the whole system deeply imprinted in my mind while the other guys, who didn't teach it, mostly remember the later stuff, while forgetting much of the earlier details and techniques.

11 - THE STAR WARS CONNECTION

When the Star Wars movie came out, it was a sensation. At the time I was a member of the old AOL Taoism message board. It was different from the others because it was a secret message board. AOL programmers had forgotten to list it, or put in a link to it. Only those who were invited and given the link were able to participate.

One of the members mentioned they saw similarities between the Jedi, the Force, and Taoism. At first I didn't see it, and I thought not, but then the senior member of our little forum (and a mentor of mine), disagreed. This guy was a very old Taoist who liked to write about the wonderful visits he was having with his great great grandnieces in the United States, and of going snowmobiling in Vermont in the woods in wintertime. I do believe he was a Taoist immortal. His screen name was Liu I Ming and he was so old and so wise that I thought perhaps it could be the same person. This old Taoist, whoever he was, was friends with the late Joseph Campbell, who was an advisor to George Lucas. Liu I Ming and Campbell discussed many of the points of the movies together, so he had a lot of insider information. Mr. Ming said that prior to the last three movies and before the remade versions of the first three were released, that some Taoists got together with Lucas and got him detoxed from some of the fanciful ideas he'd gotten from Campbell. Accordingly, these later movies show a more accurate version of the Taoist masters being represented by the Jedi. They offer a more accurate rendition of some of their Chi Kung training methods and way of life. Therefore, Star Wars is not only a first class warrior story, it uses Chi Kung masters as models for their heroes ... and villains.

The far out abilities displayed in the movies are a bit of an exaggeration in places, but they are a fairly accurate portrayal of abilities which have been cultivated by only a very few of the most advanced masters. However it is not so difficult for most of us to cultivate some of those abilities to a lesser extent if we do the right exercises. To be specific, the Jedi represent Nei Kung masters, and the Force represents chi.

Following is an explanation of some parts of the movie that are representative of some abilities derived via training in the Taoist spiritual path of the warrior.

In the first movie, Obe Wan Kenobi finds Luke Skywalker lying on the ground after being hit in the head with a club. He puts his hand on Luke's forehead, and then tells R2D2 that Luke is OK. He is doing healing energy work on Luke. Chi Kung masters can be very effective at doing energy healing work on others.

In the bar fight scene in the first movie it shows Obe Wan dealing with two attackers. The second one got his arm cut off, but the first one is casually pushed, goes flying off to the side at high speed, and crashes into an immovable object with a loud bang. This type of pushing is straight out of Tai Chi, the Taoist martial art which is also a type of Chi Kung. The attacker who was pushed would have been hurt more than the one who had his arm cut off. This kind of pushing also comes from the ability to push others with energy, without touching, which is often portrayed in the Star Wars movies. Actually, it works better at closer range.

The casual, informal way that they dress and act towards each other and strangers is typical of Taoists. Teachers and students are learning together, they also learn from each other, and there are no ritual acts of formality, such as bowing. There are no ranks or belts or graduations within Taoist Chi Kung (excludes religious Taoism). All are students. The only thing that matters, and the only way rank can be determined, is by who has the most chi power (has the most Force in them), because chi power is the goal, the golden carrot that we seek. This was represented by the way Obe Wan and Darth Vader talked to each other about who was the most powerful just before their last duel.

Taoist masters were often hermits, wandering in the wilderness such as Obe Wan and Yoda. But sometimes they were advisors to emperors, such as Lao Tzu and Darth Vader. Possibly there was one Chi Kung master who was also an Emperor. This would be the legendary Yellow Emperor of China.

The ancient Chinese Yellow Emperor was a benevolent kind of master, but the Star Wars Emperor was a Sith, a master who had been recruited by the dark side.

When Obe Wan, and later Yoda, are training Luke Skywalker, they tell him several times to feel the Force, to listen to the Force. This illustrates the foundational principle in learning to work with energy, and that is learning to feel it. You learn to feel it in yourself, in your environment, and in others. This type of thing was demonstrated when Luke is shown practicing sword fighting while blindfolded, and when Obe Wan and Darth Vader knew who and where each other were, when their different spaceships came closer to each other. It was also demonstrated by them being aware of each other's location before they actually saw each other, just prior to their last duel. Darth even mentions this, that he could *feel* him. By this he means feel the energy, as in a tactile feeling, not as in a psychic feeling. As mentioned earlier, this same ability was demonstrated in real life by the way Andy could sense Mr. Yueng when Mr. Yueng was inside a large building, and Andy was walking by outside.

Listening to energy is the first of the three steps in energy cultivation that a person goes through as they progress slowly along the Taoist path of Nei Kung, and these are spoken of in the Tai Chi Classics. The three steps are: 1 - Listening to energy, 2 - controlling energy, and 3 - knowing energy.

Another way the movies portray Chi Kung practices is the way Darth Vader breathes. Without all the noise, of course, but the long, slow, full, deliberate breaths, without pauses (except for speaking), are the way people should always breathe, and this is taught in some Chi Kung systems. The noisy breathing was due to the mask and machinery, but that is the only way it could be demonstrated. All Jedi breathe with long slow full breaths, all the time.

Obe-Wan Kenobi, Darth Vader, Yoda, and the Emperor are all very old yet they are still strong, healthy, with youthful vitality, and full of energy. These are exactly the same goals Chi Kung has.

It is possible for an advanced practitioner to cause other people to physically move against their will. This is done without touching, only with the use of energy, and is a common objective with certain kinds of Chi Kung. It is much rarer to find a person who can cause an inanimate object to move without touching it. An advanced master can give off a sudden explosive burst of energy which can injure or possibly kill another person. This was demonstrated in the films many times by Darth Vader. This explosive burst of energy can be transmitted through the air without touching but it commonly accompanies a physical strike.

Someone who is not sensitive to energy may not feel the energy shock but they will still be injured. Someone who is advanced in Chi Kung may experience pain but no injury, this was demonstrated when the Emperor was attacking Luke Skywalker on the Emperor's spaceship in one of the later movies. A true master, someone who can handle the extra energy due to their practice of handling large amounts of energy won't be injured, it will just make them stronger. Thus is why advanced masters don't use these energy techniques on each other, which is also demonstrated in the movie.

Whether the ability to push people with energy exists is a hot and controversial subject on the internet forums. With many for and many against. The fact is that *it is possible* to push people with energy. I have done it to others and I've had it done to me. The key point is that it depends on many details, and I'll get more into those details later in this book.

Keep in mind that Star Wars is an adventure movie and that energy is normally used to feel good and rarely used for fighting in real life. The primary goals of mastering energy are health, longevity, and spiritual growth, although it was definitely practiced by warriors for the sake of cultivating special abilities. Most Nei Kung practitioners prefer to lead quiet peaceful lives because it is an effective spiritual practice. For as a person advances spiritually they experience increasing synchronicity. It appears synchronicity causes you, if there is a fight, to "not be there." However, if they ever did get a bee in their bonnet and get motivated by something then they can switch from resting sleepily in a recliner and turn in to hell on wheels in half a second. As the saying goes, "It is better to be a warrior in a garden .. than to be a gardener in a war."

Another point where Star Wars films blends with Chi Kung is how many of the very advanced masters traditionally had very few students, oftentimes only one, and if more than one, it was most often one at a time. Also, those who become very advanced usually start their training at a young age. For example, when Yoda started training Luke, he lamented that Luke was too old.

When Luke Skywalker was a student of Yoda, he was shown balancing, doing a handstand while practicing levitating rocks. This is representative of the common Chi Kung practice of holding strenuous standing meditation postures while simultaneously doing energy work.

The place where George Lucas was in disagreement with Taoist philosophy, as mentioned earlier, is that people on the dark side do not have the ability to cultivate very high levels of chi power,. Evil people may be able to cultivate some kind of spirit power, but high chi power can be attained only by people of the highest ethics because of all the meditation required. In most cases, meditation, at least in the long run, will either 'cure' evil, or the evil will simply cause the person to stop meditating. An excellent self policing feature of the spiritual path, if you ask me.

There are many schools and sects within the Taoist tradition. The types of schools we are dealing with here are some of the more esoteric schools of Chi Kung, or internal alchemy, which fall under the broad umbrella of real Nei Kung. They are the spiritually oriented, powerful self improvement systems, commonly called cultivation, in the branch of Taoism sometimes called Hygiene Taoism. Most of the people in old China studied martial arts, primarily because it was a matter of survival. Most of the people who practice these esoteric energy practices are also advanced martial artists. The martial artists acquire these special psychic and energy abilities because it gives them an "unfair" advantage when it comes to self defense. So it was common for the people who were the most serious and dedicated researchers and practitioners of the Taoist internal martial arts to also cultivate special abilities. The Ninjas are a good example, because the Ninjas descended from Chi Kung masters who migrated to Japan long ago. They fought a war with the Samurai and lost, but instead of killing themselves, as was the Japanese custom, they went into hiding.

I don't like using the term martial artists so much these days because it has more of a connotation of being someone like a professional sports person. The true deadly warrior methods break all the sport rules that the competition fighters train to obey. They are designed to end a conflict in one second, so a confrontation never really turns into a "fight" anyway.

Most of the sects which teach these abilities are secret. They are difficult to find, and more difficult to get in to, and once a person gets in, they don't get out. One of the better known sects that is actually an open school, is the Dragon Gate Sect. The Dragon Gate master teaches seminars around the world. Sold out, he did, and don't expect to become one of his inner door students any time soon. This is the problem with popularity, thousands of people want in, but less than a handful can become what are called inner door students. People on this particular spiritual path are sometimes said to be on the path of the sorcerer. There is a good book on this subject : "Opening the Dragon Gate - The Making of a Modern Taoist Wizard".

12 - THE PATH OF THE WARRIOR WIZARD

A wizard is basically an advanced form of warrior. But what is a warrior?

A warrior is a person who is willing to fight for what they feel is right, not physical fighting necessarily, but moreso fighting for principles and ideals. They are willing to face the physical risk and the fear which is inherent confrontations. They feel their principles justify the risk, so they go ahead with the battle, with full knowledge of possible defeat. This is all obvious of course. So a warrior is above all, someone who is willing to face their fears instead of running away. That is a most important requirement on the spiritual path, because on it you will eventually enter a dark cave of fear and engage in the biggest battle of your life. Another way of saying that you will meet your own worst enemy.

It's pretty simple really. Warriors are the ones with enough internal fortitude to follow a fast spiritual growth. People who can tough it out through the bad parts without giving up. people who relish the challenge because it gives them another battle, which is always another chance to make more progress.

Most warriors these days are of the verbal kind, which is fine, but back in old China it was different. It was a lawless land with plenty of bandits and warring political factions. Those were dangerous times so most people practiced martial arts as if their lives depended on it, because often, they did. It's basically the same with people who learn self defense these days as well. The warrior must act as judge, jury, and executioner all rolled into one. They may have to kill, and they know just as well, that they could be killed. This makes them very aware of their own death and of the value of their life to them. They know that someday they will die and they know that day could could be any time. This awareness of death colors their entire attitude towards life, and they do not shy away from it. They take life seriously, love it, and want to stay alive very much. At the same time not taking everything else all so seriously. A similar attitude was sparked in me when I attended Alexander Everett's seminar and he explained how being dead was kind of a failure insofar as enjoying your golden years is concerned. Back then, I got the part about staying alive, but it took me much longer to get the part about not taking everything so seriously.

Warriors naturally want to become powerful, and it turns out the Taoists are in luck! While most warriors are only able to focus on becoming powerful by building physical strength and learning combat, the lucky Taoist warrior gets to learn well tested methods for increasing their psychic powers, in addition to building physical strength and learning combat.

There are three aspects to Taoist cultivation that are pretty well known. They are called Jing, Chi, and Shen ... which translate as vitality, energy, and spirit.

All three of these are cultivated in Nei Kung, and they all work together. A person needs good vitality in order to be able to cultivate strong energy, and all the extra energy is used to add much faster progress to spiritual growth. Vitality comes from good strength, flexibility, and muscle tone, and there's only one way to get those things. Physical exercise. You find that going through a form of Nei Kung can be a real workout. The exercises are variable in terms of how strenuous you want to make them. Initially it is more strenuous, in order to cultivate more physical strength; later, after you get stronger, it no longer feels strenuous.

The ancient sages of China desired youthful vitality, even into their advanced old age. For one thing, youthful vitality and mobility give a warrior that extra bit of advantage in battle, but mainly it just helps an old man get around joyfully and without pain or age related disabilities. Vitality powers the energy engine, which powers the spiritual engine, so real Nei Kung is a lot of exercise ... followed by sitting meditation ... which is also strenuous.

The good news is that most of the exercises which are so effective for increasing psychic powers are also effective for increasing longevity via vitality. Read ... bigger aura.

As you become increasingly psychic, you begin to have contact with the spirit world. Becoming more psychic is a kind of power itself, but the important thing is it makes you aware there is more, much much more to life. Quite simply, it makes your world into a bigger place. Becoming aware there really is a spirit realm and that you connected with it makes your universe a bigger place once again. The possibilities are tantalizing, the dangers are real, so it's best to just keep a low profile and meditate, be good, and don't mess with anybody in the spirit realm. There are many tricksters! As with other gifts of this nature, being psychic is neither good nor bad, it is both. Every benefit comes with its burden attached, this is inescapable. Hence the expression, "double edged sword."

Since the warrior is aware of his death and has this kind of detached lustiness for life, he calculates his life well and leads his life in a very deliberate fashion. Warriors instinctively know what is important to them. The awareness of death gives a person clarity which allows decision making without regret. What's more, his decisions are usually strategically correct, so he relishes life's challenges. He fully understands all his choices are his responsibility and once he makes them there is no time for recriminations or regret. Knowledge of his death makes him aware such sentiments are of no practical use. His death advises him how to choose strategically, and how to live with virtue for its own sake. The warrior has enormous patience, he waits ... there is no rush because he knows he's only waiting for his determination and will power.

Once the warrior becomes mature enough to establish strong will, and this will is based on post-enlightenment clarity, he gets to a point where unexpected things begin happening in his life. Amazing things start to happen. These may well go unnoticed at first, but after a while the adept realizes there is just too much of this synchronicity going on to write it off as pure chance. Something big is happening, and you notice your will and sometimes your wishes begins to manifesting more often. This speaks to a much bigger piece of the mystery. How is synchronicity even possible? It's a truly amazing thing!

This is another place where the Taoist Nei Kung adept receives a big benefit from the energy work he learns and which is so lacking in other systems, because it appears that the bigger your aura gets, the more special abilities you acquire. In Taoism these are called special abilities, and you may think of it as plain old magic. However, much of it can be more or less scientifically ascribed to having significant chi power, and being able to work with energy. For example if you have chi power in your hands they are more effective at healing. If you have chi in your belly, it gives you good health, physically and emotionally. It also helps to keep you centered, grounded, and warm. Having more chi in your heart will make you more emotional in both positive and negative ways.

If a person has a lot of chi in their head, that will make them more psychic. Having too much energy in your head can also make you a little bit crazy and over emotional. Now, for a hermit living alone on a mountaintop, somewhere out in nature, to be highly emotional is one thin ... but for a stressed out, poisoned, city slicker to be highly emotional and a bit crazy can make life difficult to say the least. For some reason I always gravitated towards working on more energy in my head. After my hands it was my head that became sensitive to energy. I was hoping that being wiser would help guide me along my own path of Tien Shan Chi Kung, because when there are thousands of techniques a person naturally tends towards practicing some over others and I thought the extra wisdom and insight would help advise me as to which techniques would be better for me to focus on, in order to make the best progress.

There is another great wisdom in Tien Shan Chi Kung which I have seen in no other Chi Kung system and it is the way it focuses on fast spiritual development by first focusing on more exercises which make the hands powerful with chi. Once the hands are powerful with chi they become much more effective tools at increasing the chi power in your body, first in the belly and then throughout the body. Mr. Yueng had us concentrate on this stage of increasing the chi in our bodies and making our auras ever bigger for around four years or more. With all our high power methods, plus the big weekly energy boost and cleaning from the master, our bodies and hands were bright with chi. Our whole bodies buzzed with the delicious energy of life. This is when we began to focus more on our heads, and use our powerful hands to direct the energy in our bodies up to our heads. So, you see, this is a very fast and effective method. The spiritual path of the wizard needs to be a fast path because there is so far to go. That is the neat thing about real Nei Kung … it can take you all the way to the mountain top. There is a saying: "some paths meander around the base of the mountain and drop you off at some other path. Some paths go up into the foothills, where there are better views of the mountain top, and they wander around there before dropping you off some cliff or at some other path. Then there are a few paths which take you straight from the foot of the mountain to the top." Which one do you want? Some are not ready for a fast path, because the fast path is the most challenging, You will have to face your own worst enemy sooner than many are ready to do. Fast is efficient, and fast and efficient is yet another form of power of the system itself, in addition to the power with which it imbues the practitioner.

I think now is a good time to point out that all this power I speak of is generally unused. Our goal was not to use this energy, but to retain it in our bodies in order to build it up to higher and higher levels. A practitioner doesn't go around power tripping on other people with his energy. The path really isn't meant for those who want to have power over others, so those who become entranced by some meager abilities get sidetracked into a detour and basically stop evolving in a holistic way. They may continue to evolve somewhat along their chosen path, but it is still a detour. There are many detours. Each special ability that a person acquires becomes a potential detour. The reason we don't want to give energy away when we are in the early stages is simply because it allows us to grow stronger and evolve further, more quickly. Once a person has emotionally matured with their ability, they can choose how to use it in a more ethical manner. The longer a practitioner waits before giving it away, determines how far they can go with chi cultivation. It's up to the individual. Some start giving it away right away, like my student who became an energy healer. Other people who cultivate chi power wait forty years before doing healing, long after having their enlightenment experience. At this point they can have ossibly acquired healing abilities bordering on the miraculous. So it's up to the practitioner. They can stop advancing and start giving it away any time they want, it is entirely their choice.

One of the major benefits of a fast path like real Nei Kung is that it brings you to enlightenment very fast compared to most other practices. After the enlightenment experience is when things really start happening. The enlightenment experience itself is closely linked to energy cultivation methods. For example, in Hindu yoga it is called the kundalini experience, which is when the energy rises up a person's spine to their head.

There is a fundamental difference between the enlightenment experience in Hinduism and Taoism. In Hinduism, in general of course, they work on amplifying the energy at the base of the spine to such a high level that it blasts its way upwards to the head. This can cause some serious difficulty as the energy blasts its way through all the blockages. Some people have a real hard time with the physical aspects of it alone.

In Taoism, on the other hand, the student works on getting the energy to flow all over the body, up and down, side to side, every which way, and this helps to energetically reduce or remove blockages. Because the energy flows back down, and the person is grounded and healthy from his Chi Kung practice, then enlightenment is a much easier experience. It's just as powerful, but more peaceful, and the emotional bliss is accompanied by some physical bliss as well. Therefore in Taoist systems, enlightenment tends to be a hugely pleasant experience, while in Hinduism and Buddhism it can be brutal, painful, and scary.

This is why it is wise if those Hindus also do physical yoga, and don't just sit all the time. If the body is in better condition, then enlightenment will be less problematic.

Concerning body conditioning, the Tai Chi classics say the sage's body is like steel wrapped in cotton. This means their muscles are soft but their bones are hard, which is the opposite of normal aging. Lao Tzu wrote essentially the same thing in the Tao Te Ching.

Many people are attracted to Nei Kung because they see demonstrations of special abilities.

Those demonstrations are either cheap magic stage tricks, or are good examples of what a detour looks like. What is more important to you, being able to light up a teeny LED light, or living to a hundred and twenty years of age, whilst enlightened and in good condition? I'm afraid many of those who are attracted to the Way by these kinds of demonstrations are doomed to failure because they are motivated by ego and social power. It really depends on the person's intent, if they want power to impress their friends at parties and make money, then it is their ego speaking. If it is because they are curious to learn how such things can work then there is hope - but they will never learn it by reading about it. The path is entirely experiential. Those who are attracted to trite demonstrations of power are more likely to be sidelined by amateurs and fundamentalists into paths which are quite limited and oftentimes even dangerous.

To me, the real power that comes from the practice are the psychic abilities it can convey. To know what is going on around you, to know what people are thinking, to feel what other people are feeling, to know what is going to happen, those all add up to a kind of power that can be much more beneficial and useful than being able to stand on one leg while someone tries to push you over, for example.

I started finding out how psychic Mr. Yueng was. He never said anything like, "I know what you're thinking," he just demonstrated in in a perfectly casual manner.

Mr. Yueng loved to eat out at different Chinese restaurants, and Seattle had some good ones. So we often got together in the evening at some restaurant of his choice. He was a master of Chinese food, having worked for a long time as a head chef in Ruby Chow's luxury Chinese restaurant in Seattle. Usually we went to dinner with Mr. Yueng, his wife, Angela, Larry, and I. my wife came along a couple of times as well. When I was preparing to go to our first dinner together I put on the Rolex watch my dad gave me as a graduation present. Once it was on I thought, "no, this is to flashy and ostentatious," so I put my cheap old Timex digital watch on instead. My wife and I were the first ones to the restaurant after Mr. Yueng and Angela. He was standing at the check out counter, and the first thing he did was show me his watch and say "Look, watch." He was wearing a big flashy ostentatious gold watch. I was a little spooked by that, I didn't know if it was a coincidence, or if he was making reference to what I had gone through with the watch at home.

Once, a long time ago, a friend gave me one of those big old heavy punching bags. So I hung it on a branch of the Cedar tree in the back yard. It hung there for months, and I didn't try hitting it till it had been there for a while. I'm not really into punching that much anyway, as I prefer softer methods. I hit it a few times to try it out, and didn't like it. When I went to class the next week Mr. Yueng told me that if I hit something like a punching bag hard, when the impact is made it causes a shock wave, a reflection of the punch, to travel back up your arm and into your body where it can damage internal organs. So I gave the punching bag to a charity.

Because I worked at home, I enjoyed spending time landscaping the front yard. People really seemed to appreciate those efforts. One person who came to the house after I had been working on the front yard for some years remarked it was like an enchanted garden. There was a giant clay pot full of wet dirt in the front yard, and I wanted to move it. So I straddled it, and bent over to pick it up. Suddenly, I thought that was a bad idea because I had a small hernia, and that posture is the one that causes hernias. So instead, I stood to one side of the big pot, twisted and bent over sideways, and picked it up that way. The next week in class I asked Mr. Yueng if there was any Chi Kung that can heal a hernia and he said no. But then he bent over in exactly the same position I had been in when I'd picked it up, and he said, "but if you pick up something heavy like this you can break your back." So he had seen me do it, and he knew why I did it too. I imagine he was somewhat alarmed when he saw me pick it up, for fear I might hurt myself. He lived around twenty miles away in South Central Seattle while I lived in North Seattle, and I very much doubt he had a spy watching me all the time.

After Mr. Yueng retired from teaching us, my chi kung brother, Larry, started coming over once a week and we would practice Chi Kung together. One week I would lead and he would follow, and the next week he would lead and I would follow. We alternated back and forth each time. Since there are so many thousands of techniques we had a lot of different things to explore together and we ranged far and wide over the system. We really learned a lot this way, because we would remind each other of long lost techniques and then see how it better connected with the whole. For example, once I recalled something I had forgotten about which M.r Yueng had only done once in class. Out of the eight years I was with him he did a few things only once. If a student was not paying attention or if he didn't practice it right away and forgot about it, then it would be gone forever. I recalled it during our practice and so I did it. The next week it was Larry's turn to lead and he had been playing with it at home. He did the same thing I had done but he expanded on it with some variations. I then evolved some more logical variations of it and showed them to Larry

Steve Gray

the following week. In this way, by going back and forth and feeding off each other's insights we discovered this thing Mr. Yueng had done only one time in eight years held the keys to a whole spectrum of secret high power techniques related to what is called "energy packing."

By the way, what most practitioners think of as energy packing is hilarious. Someone did a damn good job of hiding the goods with that one!

Larry was a train driver who worked the night shift, so he would come over in the afternoon to practice, and he always brought a joint with him. Marijuana, by the way, is the medicinal plant of choice of the ancient sages and Chinese shamans. Aside from being the miracle youth drug with all its medical benefits, marijuana also relaxes you and makes your muscles relaxed and softer. Having softer muscles enables more energy flow, causing you to feel that much more energy. It allows you to learn new things about energy, that you otherwise might not, due the extra sensitivity bestowed by the plant.

I'm a Taoist, but he is a Christian, not a fundamentalist but moreso like a Christian mystic. The mystics of most different religions usually see eye to eye pretty much but, the fundamentalists of those different religions generally do not.

He and I were sitting around smoking our joint in

the practice room one day, and Larry started to talk about Jesus. He was telling me about how the second coming of Jesus was near, and how the chosen ones would be saved and rise into heaven, while the unchosen ones would be left behind to rot in their cities. What's funny is it turns out that the ones who are chosen are the ones who believe Jesus will come back to get them. Well that looks kind of like circular reasoning to me. I don't have much use for beliefs, but I'm also not the kind of guy that wants to be left behind, you know, just in case.

So I voiced the question in my mind, "Mr. Yueng, is this true?" Right away the answer came back: "Bu-shit!" which is exactly how he used to say bullshit at home, without the 'L' sound. That way I found out he was watching us all the time and he could use telepathy whenever he wanted to. He had been listening the whole time. He used to reserve the bullshit label mostly for all the wimpy fundamentalist Chi Kung practices that are out there taking over the Chi Kung scene. I didn't tell Larry what Mr. Yueng's answer had been, until many years later.

I'll tell you a little bit about the word 'believe.' The word believe means "do not know." When you say "I believe" you may wish something is true, or logically assume something is true, but you really aren't sure. If you knew something you would say you know it, but when you say you believe something you are saying that you do not actually know it.

When people go around saying: "I believe this, I believe that, I believe the other thing" they are really saying: "I don't know this, I don't know that, I don't know the other thing."

Another time, I was sitting alone in my practice room and had just smoked my pipe. I stood up to do some Chi Kung and suddenly became all emotional. I started crying, and saying "I'm sorry I'm not a good student." I envisioned myself as a failure because I didn't think I was making any progress, and I felt guilty about not spending enough time meditating. This feeling of unworthiness is something that has been with me throughout life but it's fading away now. Right away I heard Mr. Yueng, he said, "It's okay, don't worry about it." Then he went on to explain in more detail, but the last part of it faded away from my hearing because I started thinking, "wow this is telepathy." As always, when thinking starts, awareness diminishes, so his explanation kind of trailed off slowly and faded away. The interesting thing about telepathy is that it translates for you. Mr. Yueng spoke very little English, and when he did speak you could see that he only knew the simplest phrases. I'm sure he could understand it a lot better than he could speak it ... particularly considering his psychic abilities of knowing a person's situation and thoughts. During the telepathy though I was hearing perfect english, however with Mr. Yueng's voice. Therefore it isn't the actual words that get transmitted telepathically, it's the wordless idea that precedes the spoken word, and anyone from any language will be able to understand any other language speaker by using telepathy.

This is also something that Lao Tzu referred to in his Tao Te Ching when he explained that the sage teaches without speaking. There are two ways this is done. One is that telepathy and "psychic leading" can be done without spoken words, but even more so it means that the master keeps his yap shut while leading a class. The more you see a Chi Kung teacher using spoken words to teach, the more you know he is either an amateur, or he has no interest in creating adepts.

Teaching without speaking also relates to the master not telling his student how to lead his life. Teacher's advice was usually along the lines of health related issues or details about a certain movement. There was never a word about religion, beliefs, what to think, or what to do. A big part of it included not telling the student how the Nei Kung works. Rather, requiring the student figure it out for himself. That's how you create a master. Babysitting someone with all kinds of advice does not a master make.

If you do the right kind of Nei Kung it gradually causes the bone sutures at the top of your head to open right at the crown point, the seventh chakra, like in a newborn baby. However that can be taken a step further. Once a Tibetan Lama went cruising through our area and held a little seminar. The seminar was only for a few advanced masters, and the goal was do the meditations and chi kung needed to get the skin at the top of the head, right above the already open bone sutures, to open up. During this retreat they all meditated together and were not permitted to wash their hair or scratch their heads. Mr. Yueng said he was the first of them to have it happen, and it took him about eight days. They had to stay until all of them achieved this, and those who achieved it first, did energy work on the later ones to help speed them up. He said at first a sort of pimple forms on the crown point of the head, and then it pops open. When it opens, the teacher inserts a piece of straw into the master's head. Wheat straw, not drinking straw. It goes in about two inches, and there is no pain. Mr. Yueng showed me some pictures that were taken of him when he had the straw in his head and you could see it clearly. He said when the straw is inserted it is like a radio antenna. Actually it was like being tuned into a news radio station 24 hours a day, and that 99% of the news was bad, and he didn't like it. He tried to turn it off by eating steaks and smoking cigars, but it didn't turn off.

I read a book about Tibetan practices that told about them taking a promising person, operating on their heads to insert a sliver of wood, causing them to become super psychic. Mr. Yueng said that was not true and that it had to happen naturally, from the inside out, like it did for him.

Because of this and via other experiences I had with him, I would say Mr. Yueng was omniscient. To me, omniscient does not mean knowing everything in the universe all at the same time, but rather, knowing whatever information it is that they need to know or are curious about. Basically, being able to find the answer to whatever question they may have at any given moment. I discovered it the time Mr. Yueng and I were talking about all the doomsday scenarios surrounding the 2012 'end of the world' non event. I knew the world couldn't end, but I did think there might be some catastrophe, like maybe the economy crashing, which appeared to be right around the corner every moment.

Mr. Yueng said, "Many will die." Kind of alarming, because, if anything, he was a master of understatement. I asked him how they would die, and he said he didn't want to know, which means if he did want to know that the answer would come to him. But he didn't want to know, and that was fine. I myself find there is more and more that I care less and less about knowing.

Lao Tzu wrote about this ability in the Tao Te Ching when he explained that the sage can sit in his room, and know what is going on in the world. Beginners naturally take this to mean the sage knows what is going on simply because he is so aware of this happy disaster called human nature. That masterfully written book, the Tao Te Ching (TTC), has different levels of meaning. from shallow to deep, and those who are more aware, have more experience, and are wiser ... will see deeper meanings. Then, as you make your progress along the Way, you are able to notice when you reach the different signposts left behind for us by the ancient sages. Sitting in your room and knowing what is going on in the world is essentially telling us about the super psychic abilities of high level Chi Kung masters, of which Lao Tzu was one.

This omniscience of his included what he could sense with energy with his hands. He could scan your body by connecting to the energy coming through your hands, and he would feel in his body what you felt in your body. This is real empathy. His energy was so clean and pure and he was so sensitive to his own energy that he could feel your discomfort or pain in his own body. Whatever it was, stomach ache, head ache, sprained knee, he could feel your energy and feel your pain. He also had an uncanny ability to trace the cause of a problem to its root. In this way he could do an extraordinary job of finding what needed healing.

He healed my wife, who had a bad sinus infection, in twelve hours. She had taken three rounds of different antibiotics to cure the sinus infection and none worked. It kept getting worse, plus the medicine itself caused her to have other problems, particularly with digestion. She was desperate, so she accepted when I asked her to go see Mr. Yueng. She didn't believe in any of that energy healing stuff but I talked her into going by saying lets just try it out, it cant hurt. So we went that evening after she got off work. Mr. Yueng scanned the energy around her upper body with his hand about a foot away, he used it to locate a couple of swollen glands in her neck. He showed me how to gently massage these glands, and additionally he did a little energy work on her. The next morning my wife was fine. She had absolutely no symptoms of her sinus infection, but she did have something new, a bladder infection. I had a class the next day so I told Mr. Yueng about the new problem. He rolled his eyes and told me to bring her in again, so I did. This time he did most of the energy work on her lower body. When I say energy work, I mean that it is done without touching; it is not physical in any way. The next morning her bladder infection was gone. It was obvious to me that Mr. Yueng had healed a real bad sinus infection that a lot of antibiotics couldn't touch and then healed a bladder/kidney infection. Imagine then, my shock, when I casually mentioned him healing her sinus infection six months later and she denied that he had healed her. This shows the amazing blinding effect that *belief* can have on any poor soul.

Mr. Yueng could scan your energy and feel the condition of the marrow in your bones. As people age their bone marrow changes to fat, and Mr. Yueng described it as the healthy young bone marrow feeling juicy, and the old fatty bone marrow feeling dry. He could feel the energy from far away too, for example when he first met my future Kung Fu teacher, Dave Harris, Dave was standing at the back of a classroom. When Mr. Yueng came to the door he could feel something strange about Dave's bones that he couldn't identify. Later when he came in, he saw Dave had a lot of bone calluses on his forearms. These were the result of bone microfractures from hitting the wooden Wing Chun dummy so hard. Mr. Yueng laughed when he found out what was causing the strange bone signal.

Once I took a student to him. She was a thin delicate yin vegetarian type of lady, the kind that is very sensitive to energy. He had her sit in a chair at his little round table and stood to her side. He put one hand about eighteen inches behind her back, at heart level, with the hand open. He then placed his other hand about eighteen inches in front of her heart with that hand closed. When he opened the hand in front her jaw dropped open. He blasted her heart with more energy than she would ever have been able to imagine. So you can see, Mr. Yueng liked to use a little bit of showmanship and have some fun.

Once, in Chi Kung class it was only me there along with this very psychic Russian guy whose name I forgot. He had been a student for around a year. We were standing around talking with Mr. Yueng, when suddenly he decided to give us a demonstration of how to take sick energy out of your liver. He was standing about twelve feet away from the two of us and he put his right hand about two inches from his liver with the fingers in a bird beak hand posture like he was reaching into his liver and stood there for some ten seconds. The Russian student said, "Look, he's really concentrating." Then Mr. Yueng moved his hand quickly about one inch towards us in a little jerking or yanking motion. When he did that I felt like I got hit by a pressure wave from an explosion. The Russian guy said, "Wow, did you feel that?!" I didn't say anything.

High level masters that like to stay hidden, will typically show you only one percent of what they can do, but there was one time when Mr. Yueng did claim a specific ability. He said if someone wanted to attack him that he could send energy from his head, and here he pointed to his head top, to his attackers's head, and he pointed to the imaginary attackers head top. Then he said, "and he no can move." In other words, he could paralyze an attacker with mind control ... he wouldn't even need to point his hands at him. I didn't doubt him for a moment.

Once I went to a rock and crystal show with Mr. Yueng, and the wife showed up with her mom and dad, who was a rock and crystal hound. Her sister and brother and law, and their two kids came along. One of the nephews, named Jon, who was around ten at the time, met Mr. Yueng. Jon was kind of entranced, maybe because of things I had told him. Mr. Yueng took Jon's hand and turned it so their hands were facing, palm to palm, and we stood there like that for three or four seconds. Then some people came along and we had to break it up, because we were blocking the aisle. Right away my nephew took his coat off. Mr. Yueng didn't say anything, but later that night I felt uncharacteristically tired, and even more tired the next day. That's when I realized he had taken a bunch of my energy and transferred it to Jon, which is why the kid took his coat off. He got so hot, so fast, and he whipped his coat off at such high speed, that in retrospect it made me laugh.

I learned greatly from many instances like that,

without a word being spoken. You can take people's life energy if you want to, or you can give them life energy if you want to. In our school it is considered very unethical to take other people's energy, and we're all so damn ethical, you know. It was okay for Mr. Yueng to take my energy though, because the reason I had so much energy to begin with was all because of him and his energy. Jon was family, and in our tradition you can do healing work on your own family. I think maybe Mr. Yueng was trying to get me to understand the feeling in my hand and/or body, when someone else is taking my energy.

Once, I was in class and there were three other students. I stood towards the back of the middle garage bay and this other guy stood in front of me. He was a cigar smoker, and had a bit of a cough during that class. He coughed a couple of times and it bothered me. The third time he was about to cough, I could tell, by the way his breathing changed. In my mind I reached out to his throat and did something like flipping a switch, and his impending cough disappeared. After that the new guy didn't cough any more in class. I also observed that Mr. Yueng had noticed me do it.

Pushing People with Energy

As noted previously, this is a controversial subject with many both for and against the idea it is even possible. For those who are self honest, experience trumps beliefs every time. So it is that I'm aware you really can push people with energy, as I explained in the chapter about the Jedis. However, the devil is in the details. There are different levels to this. The lower levels, which is what you see demonstrated by amateurs on Youtube, requires that both the teacher and the student are sensitive to chi, but more important is that they have worked with and are *sensitive to chi as pressure*. It also requires that the student cooperate, they want to experience the push, so they allow it to happen, they want it to happen. This is why you can see videos of some master who can push his students, but then when the news-team comes by to check it out, we find that the teacher can't push them, (much to his surprise). When the teacher and student have developed more of the chi power as pressure then it *is possible to push people who are resisting the push*. The most advanced masters do not need to use their hands because they are able to move energy outside their bodies with mind control alone. This is something we work on in the higher levels of Tien Shan Chi Kung.

Then of course there are the fakes, and there are plenty of them to be found. The worst one that comes to mind is some guy whose I forget, but it sounds something like Lama Dorje Dumbdrop. The fakes advertise their stuff very showily so they can attract a lot of students who want to do it too. This creates a powerful environment of suggestibility. Dumbdrop gets all his students to wear red dresses, both the men and the women. He does some lame martial arts demonstration on a male student, who must be wearing a dress, and then starts waving his arm up and down, with or without touching the sucker. The sucker immediately starts bouncing up and down like a jackrabbit and then falling down all over the place. The reason students do this is simply because they see previous students doing it, and they think it is very cool and a sign of advancement, so they really want to do it too. Add a little lack of self honesty and you get suggestibility. In no time at all, the new student is also jumping up and down like a jackass, happily, successfully. Congratulations, he's now one of the in-crowd of the great Lama, and he worked hard to get there. Via suggestibility. Dumbdrop can even get a whole row of twelve suckers to jump up and down in unison, they are so well trained.

Since I'm usually alone here in Ecuador, and since most beginners do not respond well to chi as pressure, I ended up playing around with it by myself.

At first I tried to push myself away from a wall with my hands about six inches away. It didn't work so well. Then I figured out how to apply the proper intent to it, and it started working better. But I was standing with my feet side by side ... I wasn't resisting the push but allowing it to happen. Often it would push me off balance, so I'd have to take a step back to keep from falling. I practiced this once in a while, and what do you know, I got better at it. I tried moving further from the wall and it still worked. Then I tried resisting the push by putting one foot behind the other. At first that didn't work so well either, but I learned to apply a little tension to certain muscle groups, and it increased the force enough to push me back. Or more often, since I had one foot in back, it would push me off balance towards one side or the other, even when I would fight to keep my balance. This is not the kind of thing you want to practice in public because people might think you crazy.

After that, I tried doing it while standing in the middle of my big practice room without facing any walls, and I found out that it still worked, very strange, weird, and wonderful!! That IS weird ... you can push on empty space, or push yourself by pushing on empty space, or said better, *by pushing on the energy field of the Earth*. Maybe that's not it, or if it is, then it's breaking the laws of physics again, because those laws clearly state that one energy field cannot block or push on another energy field, they flow right through each other and continue on their way undisturbed. It's a big mystery, seeing The Mystery. It's strange how it works, and it definitely requires the use of mind and intent. For example if I just make a pushing motion at random without focusing or using intent, then it doesn't influence me in the slightest. I sometimes spread my arms wide and open my hands with palms facing forward, then open my fingers, and then imagine long fingers like the long wing tip feathers of a big bird. If I focus on those things correctly and then press forward with my fingertips even a fraction of an inch it pushes me off balance if I have my feet side by side. If I chose to resist the push by putting one foot behind the other, then I need to move my fingers a little further and exert a bit of pressure, that will push me off balance. At first it makes me wobbly as it tries to push me off to one side or the other,I fight to maintain my balance, and if I relax the push, I'm able to keep my balance. Once it worked really well, and I had to jump two feet back and to the side to catch my balance.

The way this works is not that it creates any actual physical pressure. The way it works is that the mind of the person getting pushed feels the energy field of the earth in which his body is located moving, and his body instinctively wants to stay located in what it feels is the same spot. However that 'same place' is moving, due to the influence and intent of the pusher, someone who can feel himself moving through the energy field of the Earth as he walks along. This shows evidence of a direct mind link between the pusher and the pushee, and the more power the pusher has, the less the pushee needs to be aware of such things for it to work. The mind and nerves of the Jedi, as well as his sense of balance, makes him instinctively want to remain unmoving within that moving bit of space. It's all effortless, the pushee has no sense of the moving, and just goes along with it. Of course, doing it to yourself naturally raises questions of ethics, self honesty, and suggestibility. As far as I can tell with my (scientifically inspired) methods, I am not fooling myself. Besides which, I had it done to me. Once, one of my teachers who happened to be high up in the CIA, caused my head to move two feet to the left rather quickly, followed by my body of course, and I felt no pressure, no push, no movement. I just went that way, and when my visual and auditory balance feedback system kicked in, it prompted me to take a big step to catch my balance.

Due to this, I seriously doubt if sitting in a chair which is on wheels and then pushing against the fabric of the universe will move me, but what the heck do I know? If I could push myself while sitting in a chair on wheels, wouldn't that be something? Then I could join the circus with the other teachers who like to show off useless tricks. It would be neat if it did work though, because then instead of pushing myself rearwards with hands facing forward, I could push myself upwards with hands facing downwards. TAA DAA ... levitation! Sorry folks, it doesn't work that way, at least not for me. Mr. Yueng confirmed the existence of levitation, but he said it was too slow, it wasted a lot of energy, and it served no useful purpose. Although he did teach us the technique to practice in order to work on it.

So, to wax poetic about it, you could say the Force doesn't move you directly, instead it moves your spirit, and your body follows your spirit. It is proper for me to practice such things, because since dragons live in the spirit realm, they have no weight. They use this method to get around, and I'm practicing for later.

Pushing people is kind of useless for self defense, because it usually doesn't end a fight unless you push them into an oncoming bus or brick wall. It just makes the attacker angrier and more careful when he comes back, so pushing people with energy is normally a silly game ... unless you are a CIA agent and want to upset someone's balance at just the right moment without touching them. A couple of brothers who practiced together and focused a lot more on the Jedi stuff, told me about a couple of things that they had discovered. One told me if he focused on someone who could be some distance away that he could make the energy in their heart run backwards and they would die of a heart attack. Now some people may wonder how he knows that, if he never tried it. Some day, when you see a bird in a tree and you try your energy technique on it, and it falls down dead, then you know you're onto something, but that's not how it happened. He told me he thought of a new energy self defense method and was going to try it out on one of his brother's necks during a self defense class. Then he thought he should play it safe and test it out first, so he used the mental energy technique that creates a field of energy moving in a certain complex way in a spot down near the floor. Then he kicked that spot and it broke three bones in his foot.

Another brother told me about a time he went to a certain city to give a self defense seminar, and one of the participants invited him to stay at his home while there. It turned out the guy invited him because he wanted to test him in person. He wanted to attack him in his living room. Well my brother was tired from teaching all day and he said no. So then his host got up and started coming at him while my brother reclined in a big old soft chair. Without moving or pointing, my brother attacked the guy's belly with this energy technique and the foolish host collapsed on the floor in agony, holding his gut. The next day the host went to work and upon his return he told my brother, "You know, I've been thinking all day about that thing you did last night and it never happened!" Once again, such is the power of belief over self honesty. How could the guy even think or talk about "that thing," if he had never experienced it?

Such things are similar to the occasion I reached out with my mind to my fellow student's throat, and switched off his cough. It also happened when I influenced a little kid in the school hallway to stop crying by removing his stress. However, these brothers can do it at will and I did it more or less by accident, and haven't practiced such things since.

Another hugely impressive thing about Mr. Yueng and Tien Shan Chi Kung is that when he was seventy-eight, he went to an open house at the University of Washington Hospital and got a free EEG brain wave scan. The doctors interpreting the readout said his EEG was like that of a teenager's. Now that is special, and it's amazing. hat is the real valuable fruit of the practice, health, youthfulness, and longevity.

I had some other strange experiences. Some time after I 'graduated' and Mr. Yueng retired from teaching, I had a series of disturbing dreams four nights in a row. The dream was of me cutting up a body and putting the pieces down the disposal. I didn't see much of the body itself, just the smaller pieces that I was putting down the disposal. I knew it was a body of a person I had killed. This was obviously disturbing to me and I wondered how the hell I could have such dreams. A couple of years later I found out, because it was in the news. A Washington State ferry boat captain was going to court for murdering his wife and disposing of her down her own kitchen disposal. I had somehow psychically linked to the murderer and I was seeing what he was seeing through his eyes, while he was saying goodbye to his ex wife bit by bit.

Later is when more of the magic started happening. This is not at all like the kind of magic where people cast spells and say arcane prayers. It's more along the lines of simply having your wishes come true, and such things often take the form of synchronicity or premonitions.

For example: The land I got here in Ecuador is not so far from the nearest power line, which is down in the valley outside our 'crater'. It was difficult to decide whether or not to go with solar or with grid power and I didn't know how to calculate solar. So I went with the grid. I also wanted to be able to run a welder, which can be really hard on batteries. The engineers put a power pole up on the ridge above and well away from the house, like I wanted, and the power then comes to the house underground. I was shocked when I saw they put one of those bright flashing red beacon lights up there. It was the worse kind of Feng Shui attack you can imagine! It was red, like an eye looking down on us from above, the constant flashing was like the Chinese water torture whenever you were outside at night. I hated it with a passion. Those warning lights are supposed to go on mountain tops, and the pole was on a ridge well below the mountain top. Besides, there were no flashing red pole lights anywhere else in the area, just mine. It's like from a hundred miles around everyone could see exactly where Stevie's house was, while theirs were well hidden in the dark. I had plans to hire some worker to go up the pole on a big ladder and paint the light black or remove it. And then, the light just quit working. Now, those lights are made to be super reliable and burn for a million years, so to have it go out right when I was pissed off enough to make it go out was a rare chance occurrence indeed.

Another example: The builder who was working on building my place was going to have a baby son some time around my birthday, so I thought it would be cool if he was born on the same day as my birthday. I didn't tell the builder about it but did keep thinking about it. Lo and behold a few days after my birthday, he told me his son was born on that day. The baby was born prematurely and had some breathing difficulty at first, due to undeveloped lungs ,so had to be put in an incubator for a while.

Now these two examples could just be coincidences, no doubt about it, but when your wishes start coming true often enough, you start to wonder what the hell is going on. It's a bit unsettling, and you realize you need to watch out what you wish for, not that I wish for much really. I'm kind of low in the "desires" department … well, other than staying healthy.

I told Mr. Yueng about the increased synchronicity and psychic premonitions I was experiencing, but that I didn't know I'd experienced a premonition till after the event actually took place. Mr. Yueng said, "You're only psychic if you know it's a premonition."

Later I acquired some ability to know when I have a premonition, and I must say, it's a good early warning system.

There are many more anecdotes from the path of the sorcerer that can be related, but those are some of the main categories. It's an amazing journey, I wouldn't have missed it for anything!

The greatest step a person can take along the path is the last one, and that is to become an immortal.

Sadly, most of Western Chi Kung has devolved into either stretching or sitting around with your finger in your nose and visualizing things. Then there's the other aspect. There are those who are impressed by the displays of chi power and believe them. Many of these displays are tricks, but some are real. The thing is that people who are attracted to the power of the disciline are basically the wrong types to be students, and teachers who display these tricks are also the 'wrong' types, because obviously, they are mainly interested in popularity and money. The real advanced masters stay hidden and are not showy with displays of power, precisely because they do not want the pain of dealing with the wrong types of people. Of course, most people will be impressed by one of these seemingly magical displays, and it is also common for most people to want to learn to do similar tricks.

These days most everyone who is attracted to the idea of having power to perform magic tricks is the wrong type of person, but in the old days this was for warriors, and warriors do have a good reason to want just those kinds of abilities.

Most of the people who go for the popularity and money are not evil people. They are simply not so advanced spiritually, which means they were probably taught systems with big chunks missing. They don't understand the intricacies of popularity vs. keeping a low profile. Sometimes the 'systems' with big chunks missing are a result of the teacher, or his teacher's, hiding things, or from the student abandoning the practice to begin teaching before they were fully baked. The popularity situation is actually the biggest problem I have with even putting this book out. Here is something that the Taoist sage Chuang Tzu wrote about displaying yourself, translated by Thomas Merton:

The Tower of the Spirit

The spirit has an impregnable tower, which no danger can disturb, as long as the tower is guarded by the invisible protector, who acts unconsciously, and whose actions go astray when they become deliberate, reflexive and intentional.

The unconscious and entire sincerity of the Tao, are disturbed by any effort at self-conscious demonstration. All such demonstrations are lies

When one displays himself in this ambiguous way, the world outside storms in and imprisons him.

Each new act is a new failure.

If his acts are done in public, In broad daylight, he will be punished by men. If they are done in private and in secret, they will be punished by spirits.

Let each one understand The meaning of sincerity, And guard against display!

He will be at peace with men and spirits, and will act

rightly, unseen, In his own solitude, In the tower of his spirit.

~ ~ ~ ~ ~

13 - THE TAOIST PATH
OF THE IMMORTAL

Here is some added perspective on Bruce's "Be like Water' saying:

> "When a man does not dwell in self, then things will of themselves reveal their forms to him. His movement is like that of water, his stillness like that of a mirror, his responses like those of an echo." ~ Chung Tzu

An immortal, in the common Asian mind, most often refers to what in the West would be called an ascended master, whatever that is. Ass ended master?

There are many types of immortals, from hungry ghosts and demons, to avatars and gods. Maybe you could say all beings in the spirit realm are immortals, I don't know. Maybe it only applies to spirits that were previously humans.

For our purposes we are most interested in the two types of immortal, commonly known as Earthly Immortal and Celestial Immortal. An Earthly Immortal is someone who lives to be very old while still being in exceptional condition, and a celestial immortal refers to the previously mentioned ascended masters. There are two or three levels of Celestial Immortal, with the highest level of immortal having a vibration so high that not even gods can see them. Closer to the light, you might say. Mr. Yueng is definitely on that path. A very capable channeler who came to visit, told me his vibration was too high and that he could no longer communicate with this level. That is why I think that Mr. Yueng may not even be a dragon any more, but has transitioned beyond that. I'll find out some day.

The process of becoming an immortal can be described in terms of stillness and movement. Movement is important because Taoists know how much the body influences the mind and emotions, plus they are warriors, right? We learn to move as a way to meditating, meditating on the movement, which is stillness within movement. Moving exercises are also required to cultivate chi. Stillness means the quietness of a non thinking mind at first; when we do sitting or non moving meditation by focusing on the energy moving in our bodies then that is movement within stillness of the body.

Stillness is the essence of life, and movement is life itself.

Mentally, stillness is pure awareness and movement is thought. Thinking and awareness are mutually exclusive, the more a person is thinking the less they will be aware of their environment because the awareness is consumed by the thinking. When a person is carefully observing something non verbally then that is pure awareness, pure meditation, when thoughts and words about what one is observing begin to surface, then awareness has already diminished.

Many teachers beat around the bush, but Mr. Yueng came right out and said it at the beginning: "NO THINKING!"

In the beginning, with sitting meditation, the best that can be hoped for are brief periods of mental quiet and non thinking, followed by the usual choo choo train of silly thoughts that keep coming around repeatedly on their circular track. The Monkey Mind. Later, gradually, these spaces between thoughts become longer. The thoughts that come up are almost always about something you did, something you said, something you need to do, something someone said to you or something you want to say to someone, and this goes on for a long time. Then after some years the spaces between thoughts gets longer, and the thoughts that do surface are more disturbing. You remember extraordinarily embarrassing things that have happened to you, or you remember times when you did something bad to someone. It should bring up a feeling here, and the feeling we are looking for is remorse. Remorse is required for spiritual growth. It means you are judging yourself in a self honest way and experiencing the beginning of the game of ethics. It doesn't end at remorse. That bad feeling of remorse motivates a person to figure out why they did what they did, to understand themselves. After understanding comes forgiveness of self and other. In this process you can see the importance of internal self honesty, and you can see why those who are into denial can't do it. This is how you cleanse your karma.

The spaces between thoughts get longer still.

Once you do this for a few years or a few decades you may well have your enlightenment experience, and then the fun really starts.

After enlightenment, the next goal is to quiet your mind so you increasingly experience non thinking in your day to day activities. This goal or process comes naturally to some at least, they don't need to be told. Once stillness of the mind is permanently established during our day to day routine, thinking can then return, because it can no longer distract a person out of clarity and stillness... into un-clarity.

Clarity. When thoughts return to stillness, this is called stillness within movement of the mind. This takes much longer to achieve than stillness within movement of the body.

Clarity.

Mr. Yueng had something to say about clarity which demonstrates the viewpoint of meditation masters everywhere.

One day, after the other two students left, I was sitting with Mr. Yueng in his garage. The foundation of his garage stuck out at just the right height to make a little bench along the side near the back door. We were sitting there talking, and out of the blue he said: "You cwazy!" He wasn't referring to something I had just said but was referring to me personally. Well, that stung a little. I figured I was a pretty sane guy, so I went home with bruised feelings. While at home, I started thinking more about that, and remembering. Yes, sometimes I did some pretty stupid things for some pretty stupid reasons so yeah, maybe I *was* kind of crazy. Then I started thinking that being crazy wasn't so bad after all. I was a shy and solitary person, due to strong feelings of social inadequacy, but I was a pretty happy introvert.

The next week Mr. Yueng and I found ourselves once again sitting on that spot in the garage. As soon as the other two guys got in their cars but had yet to drive away, he said: "They cwazy!" Well that was weird, I thought they were real sane, but come to think of it I guess they were a little too jovial.

The third week the same thing happened. As the two guys drove away he said: "Evewybody cwazy, they think too much!" So there you have it folks, everybody is crazy. Uncontrolled and uncontrollable thinking is the same as insanity. I can see that, I can feel it. But it's not so bad after all, is it? Just don't expect your level of clarity to match the lofty self image you may have of it.

I tend to not ask questions when he says something like that. I don't ask questions enough is my problem, so I would just silently take those sayings home with me and ponder them over the week. Someday someone should hypnotize me so I can recall the many other things Mr. Yueng said to me, and to us as a group.

Clarity is required for the next step in the game, which is the hardest part of the Way, and ultimately becomes a person's lifelong pursuit. It is called stillness within movement in ethics, which in Chinese is termed 'Te.' This is virtue, which is otherwise described as skillful movement through life's situations while maintaining an inner calm, stillness. This is the stage of wisdom accumulation. This striving for perfection in ethics is a practice which never ends. No one is perfect, not even the immortals. As you look down that long hallway of mirrors of cause and effect it becomes more difficult to decide or to act. You learn to tread lightly. You learn to yield mentally because your physical training has trained you to yield physically.

I call it "The Game of Ethics." It's only a game because there is no requirement to play it, it's completely voluntary. I like to play this game because it is an entertaining challenge, and it also makes me feel better about myself. Another way to put it, is that I try to live without regrets.

If a person truly wishes the best for others and wants their own actions to provide the best outcome for the most people possible, this puts the motivational energies within them in accord with their conscience. The opposite of this is having an "inner knowing" that we should do something and then not doing it. This conflict is what is healed in Taoist alchemy. So real Nei Kung not only heals your body but also your mind and your emotions. Accordingly, all the forces within you have been aligned with the ethical. The result of this is that the motivation to do the right thing is automatic and is even stronger than sexual arousal.

This level of cultivation can only be achieved through the give and take of working with and interacting with others, not by sitting alone on a mountaintop. Through this process of interaction, the highest form of sensitive alertness (stillness) is achieved until all one's being is conscience and all one's energies and actions are directed towards ethical competence.

This is what "Becoming One with the Tao" means. When a person gets to this point, they lack any power contrary to the Way, and they are then backed by the power of the Way due to their complete interpenetration of the Way in virtue, Te. To some, the title of the book "Tao Te Ching" translates as," the way of power of virtue of some guy named Ching."

This leads us to the essence of the immortal, at which point life becomes the preserving of the Way and teaching the way to the Way. Then, stillness is identity with the Way ... and movement, life, becomes ethical perfection.

14 - Chi Kung vs. Nei Kung

To get some perspective on how real Nei Kung works, it will be helpful to explain what the difference is between Chi Kung and real Nei Kung. The reason the term 'real' needs to be used is because there is a lot of confusion these days about what Nei Kung is. What it boils down to is that all the Nei Kung that you see offered to the public via videos or books are a lie. They may be tiny pieces of a vast Nei Kung system, and obviously, a little piece of the whole thing is not the whole thing. The term Nei Kung has been bastardized beyond recognition by people who prefer money over truth, because once the concept of Nei Kung became discovered by the West, it became the next latest and greatest "quick 'n' easy" enchilada for people to engorge on, so the marketers arrived. One of the things which really made Nei Kung popular was publicity for some people who demonstrated abilities like lighting little LED light bulbs and starting fires with energy from their hands, ... practitioners like John Chang and Jiang Feng. However those were probably faked.

Not too many decades ago the term Chi Kung was rarely used, the common term was Nei Kung, and that's because back in those days, before there was much in the way of mass communication, the masters were few and the seekers were serious. Those who found a master would stay with them for a decade or more and learn countless techniques of working with energy, thousands of them. In fact it is said that the powerful systems of Chi Kung, which means Nei Kung, contain ten thousand techniques. Actually, the number ten thousand for the Chinese simply means "too many to count" or "everything." Nei Kung is something that a person would dedicate their life to, and go deeply into it with the goal of attaining mastery, and it was rare.

With the advent of many big cities, technology

and publicity, the public became increasingly aware of the many and profound benefits of Chi Kung. So Chi Kung became popular and Nei Kung disappeared into the background. Modern folks interested in doing Chi Kung for their health or entertainment don't really want to become masters. They don't want to learn thousands of techniques, they have other more important things to do, or so they assume. These people want to learn something simple and easy that will make them feel better. What happened is that some Nei Kung masters naturally wanted to help these people, so they picked a few exercises out of those they knew and put them together into what is called a form. A form means the same thing as a kata, or a choreography. Some forms are very simple sets of movements and others are rather complex and extended forms, like you get with Tai Chi. These masters, who created these small sets of exercises out of their vast storehouse of knowledge, want them to be effective, so they chose good exercises that they thought stood out as more helpful for beginners who don't want to spend a lot of time learning.

There is also a common trait of human nature at work here as well, which basically boils down to, "you want to save the best stuff for your friends." Even more importantly, it is natural to not want to give away secrets of power to anyone and everyone. Power is always dangerous. Power is the ability to get things done effectively. Power is also very attractive to bad people who want to use it to take advantage of others. Because power corrupts. Power doesn't corrupt everyone, just many, it easily corrupts those who don't have a strong sense of ethics. So it is also the job of the master to hold back and see what kind of person wants to learn his stuff, and for what purpose.

Since it is potentially dangerous, a master only teaches the high power techniques to a longer term student who can be watched for problems, someone who stays close. In any case, there's no reason to take high power methods out of context and give them to someone who can't appreciate what they really are. Students can only appreciate those techniques if they already have a good foundation on which to base that appreciation. It really is best to establish a strong foundation in energy circulation, self healing, and grounding so the high power techniques are safer and more effective.

Nei means internal, so the name, Nei Kung implies a more internal kind of art, but that is not to be taken too literally. In a broad sense internal means that it works with and cultivates your chi energy. There is plenty of Chi Kung that does energy work too so that isn't the point. There is also plenty of Chi Kung that has come to the West and is quite weak in energy work. Often it has devolved more into a stretching regimen. This isn't just in Chi Kung either, it's also happened in yoga. Yoga has turned into a kind of a circus, with things like beer yoga, hot yoga, naked yoga, etc. And keep in mind yoga has several decades head start on Chi Kung in the Western popular culture.

The point here is that you will never find real Nei Kung in a video or a book. Even if someone wanted to make one, it is technically impossible to teach ten thousand techniques with a video or book, or even with a lot of them. The Taoist Canon has ten thousand volumes, so it might be in there somewhere, but you would have to be able to read old Chinese to find out. Actually many secrets of cultivation are explained in the Classics, but secret code words are used for all the key words so even most Chinese people have little idea what they mean. The secret code words are basically meant for students who are already in the school and know what they mean.

Another difference between Chi Kung and Nei Kung is that Chi Kung works on energizing the more superficial energy lines, and does so one at a time. Whereas Nei Kung focuses more on the central channel and seeks to get all the energy flows going at the same time.

Chi Kung works from the outside in by working on different energy meridians to influence the central energy, which it does, but weakly. Nei kung, on the other hand seeks to greatly amplify the central energy so that it spills over into the outer channels and works all the energy flows simultaneously in order combine all the chi flows in the body. The person then "buzzes" with all their chi pulsing in unison. The energy blasts through blockages automatically, without the practitioner having to pay any attention to it.

Therefore, if the goal is self healing, Chi Kung can be best because it is simpler and directly addresses whatever problem is being worked on. Nei Kung isn't so efficient in the beginning, simply because it takes longer to learn and put the pieces together, and it also takes a while for the core energy to get strong enough to overflow and do its automatic and random healing work. It does end up covering all the bases though, which is another giant difference between Chi Kung and Nei Kung. Real Nei kung is holistic, and is developed to heal everything, physical, mental, and emotional. This makes Nei Kung better for the long term student who wants to go far and it makes Chi Kung better for those that wants some quick healing.

Going far in the realm of health is the essential first step on the road to immortality. It is possible to go much further than just being 'not sick.' Most people who are not sick assume they are healthy, but it is possible to get much healthier than that.

A scale going from low to high would look something like this:

Death
Very sick
Weak health
Not sick (healthy)
Outstanding vitality and health (catch cold rarely, mild, heal fast)
Olympic level athlete vitality (does not catch colds)
Glow in the dark

The primary focus of Nei Kung is the last three on the list, the primary focus of Chi Kung is on the first three on that list, but there is obviously plenty of overlap.

Tien Shan Chi Kung (which is really Nei Kung) concentrates the practice so it works on strength, flexibility, energy cultivation, and meditation all at the same time, eventually causing the practitioner's energy to fill even the center of the bone marrow and the spine. For this reason Nei Kung is considered superior for people who want to have both superior health and great physical prowess.

Many of the Chinese medical Chi Kung systems use the physical breath to activate the chi and many Buddhist Chi Kung practices are based on awareness of the physical breath. In Nei Kung, however, the focus is on what is called the subtle breath, which is actually the flow of energy in the body. Therefore much Nei Kung chi movement is independent of the physical breath. It is made to work regardless of how you are breathing.

Not only does Nei kKung work on strengthening, stretching, and energy cultivation all at the same time (in order to save time and get more practice in), it also drops all low power techniques and replaces them with higher power versions in order to go faster.

The ultimate goal is to go beyonds forms and arrive at the formless, wherein the practitioner achieves the inner essence of the practice and leaves the external scaffolding behind. This aspect, of arriving at the formless, is a fundamental principle of Taoist philosophy. Tai Chi, at its higher levels, also has the goal of achieving formlessness, but as it says in the Tai Chi Classics, one must first study the forms in order to potentially graduate to formlessness.

Another reason Nei Kung can not be learned from a video is that it requires the constant abilities of a powerful master to manipulate and add to the energy of the student. Obviously this can only be done in person. When a Nei Kung master or adept teaches, he radiates considerable energy outwards and some of this energy soaks into the student, amplifying the student's energy, which makes their progress much faster. Later, after the students become experts, they also start to radiate energy while practicing. This is why this kind of power cultivation system is taught indoors, or ideally in a cave full of crystals. When first the teacher and then the students start to radiate healthy energy, it soaks into the walls and the energy level in the room escalates dramatically. Then it reflects into the occupants of the room, so everyone is swimming in a thick sea of energy.

This is the same reason that a lot of regular Chi Kung is done outdoors when possible. It is because people are giving off a lot of sick energy as they heal and so being outdoors allows that energy to escape away out into the environment.

In real Nei Kung the master does energy work on the student during the sitting meditation part of each practice. Initially he helps to heal the student, and once healthy, he modifies their energy systems to better suit the goal, which is the fast cultivation of chi power and psychic abilities. Mr. Yueng said if a person practices Chi Kung without this energy boosting it could take a long time to, as he put it: "get their motor started," if ever. clearly, a person can not make much progress in Chi Kung if their motor hasn't started. Progress starts after you get "switched on," unless, of course, you just want stretching or calisthenics. Many who claim to be Chi Kung masters do not have this ability to radiate energy when they do chi kung simply because they haven't been trained in this manner of energy cultivation. Believe it or not, some of the fake masters haven't even heard of it.

Getting back to the videos and books you find which claim to offer Nei Kung. There's no doubt the exercises they show come from Nei Kung systems, but all Chi Kung comes from Nei Kung systems, so what's the difference?

Maybe that's a fine point and I'm wasting my breath, but in any case the battle has already been lost. Nei Kung now has a new definition, and if almost everyone is using that new definition then the term Nei Kung no longer means the Taoist Spiritual Path of the Wizard like it used to, so I guess I should really quit using it and give up. It seems more appropriate to call it the Path of the Wizard, because wizard is the term used to denote an advanced and powerful Chi Kung master. Advanced yogis in India can similarly be called wizards. I think most sensible people instinctively know you can't become a wizard by learning ten exercises in a weekend seminar which includes a certificate and a T shirt. If you ever see a wizard with a certificate you can be sure the world has gone to hell. The word 'wimpy' stands out here, and let me tell you, most of what is offered to the public in Nei Kung videos and books is outstanding (or you could say, pathetic) in its wimpyness. Most Nei Kung has gone the way of a lot of Chi Kung, and become simple stretching, along with a bunch of mind games.

The real stuff is out there. Try to find the most

advanced master you can get to, but avoid those who engage in "showiness," by "pushing" their students without touching them or activating small lights.

14 - MASTERS
OF THE WAY

Here I'd like to share stories about some of the old school masters I was so lucky to have as teachers. Most of them are gone now, and you don't see many of their kind any more in the modern world. As Grand Master Tchoung Ta Tchen put it: "Even the top masters of today are like hollow shells compared to masters of the recent past."

Tchoung Ta Tchen

I met Tchoung Ta Tchen through Andy Dale, who was my main tai chi teacher. Andy and some of his students went as a group to visit Tchoung up in Vacouver, Canada on some weekends. Tchoung was a grandmaster of Tai Chi, and his main claim to fame was how far he could push people through the air before they "touched down." He was so advanced there was only one other Tai Chi person on the North American Continent that was good enough to play the game of "push hands" with him, and that was master Chen Man Ching of New York, who in spite of the Chen name was a Yang style master who was well known and loved on the East Coast.

Here's a little something you probably didn't know about Chen Man Ching. He felt none of his students 'got it' and that he had been a failure as a teacher, so he stopped teaching, went back to China, and drank himself to death within six months.

Tchoung was a real serious dude. He was a general in the Chinese army, and definitely one of the old school. What made him different is that he really wanted his students to 'get' it. He really did.

He first started teaching in Seattle, in Chinatown, and since he never did learn to speak English, he had a Chinese translator there to help out. The class had been active for a few months, at which point Tchoung had taken a minute or more to explain a particular move. The translator said, "He basically said to relax." Another student there, a white guy, immediately said; "He didn't say that". Tchoung got a quizzical look on his face, then went over to talk to that guy. After that, the new guy became the translator, and that is when the teaching really started.

The lesson here is that even though the master wanted his students to learn well, the typical Chinese dude did not.

When Tchoung Ta Tchen was a Lieutenant in the Chinese army he was stationed for a while on Mt. Omei.

One cold winter day he went out to a clearing on the mountainside to practice some Tai Chi. Since it was freezing out, he was heavily bundled up. After doing Tai Chi for a while he noticed a skinny little old man sitting there watching him. Despite the freezing cold, the old man was wearing nothing but a loincloth.

When he saw him, the old man taunted him, "You're Tai Chi stiiiinks, bet you can't catch me, neeneer neener,!" So Tchoung chased him, but the old man was very nimble and was able to scoot over all the rocks and tree roots so fast that Tchoung couldn't catch him. So he gave up, and went back to the clearing to continue his practice.

The old man soon returned. This time he came over to Tchoung and said, "Hit me"

Tchoung: "No, I don't want to."

Old man: "Hit me."

Tchoung: "No."

So the old fellow started calling Tchoung and his ancestors all kinds of mean and nasty names. The outcome was predicatable.

Tchoung punched him in the stomach so hard the old man went flying back about eight feet and crashed on some big rocks. He immediately sprang up and said, 'Hit me again." So, POW, the old man went crashing onto the rocks again.

Then he came over, unhurt, and introduced himself. He was the abbott of the local mountaintop monastery, and he invited Tchoung up to practice some Chi Kung.

This was a rather common way for Taoist masters to meet in the olden days … they would trade punches to the stomach in order to see how the other handled it.

In that way Tchoung learned Mt. Omei Chi Kung, which he taught to Andy. Andy then taught it to me.

Andy once learned a different Tai Chi form, which took him a couple of month. , I can't recall which form it was, something obscure. Anyway, he showed it to Tchoung Ta Tchen. He showed it to him only one time.

After a month or so Tchoung performed the new form for Andy. He did the whole form, but he did it better, employing more of the principles of Tai Chi. So he was able to learn and incorporate the whole form, after seeing it only one time.

Going to see Tchoung was my first experience with a real live grandmaster of the internal arts. One thing he would do sometimes is have some of his better students line up in a row with their backs six feet from the wall. There were thick pads on the wall. Then he would go down the row, and one by one, he would do a little push hands with the student. The student would try to push him and he would yield out of it, and then push them. Trying to push him was like trying to catch a cloud. Getting pushed by him was like meeting the irresistible force. One of the senior students told me you couldn't really feel the push, it was like you got seduced into flying through the air, which indicates the addition of energy pushing. They would still be traveling upwards when they slammed against the pads on the wall.

Tchoung was a big old portly guy with a big belly. So I assumed it was soft pudge. Maybe he was reading my mind because one time he came over and told me to press with my thumb against his belly. Let me tell you, I can press real hard with my thumb when I brace it with my fingers. His belly was not soft at all, it was like pressing on a piece of wood. It wasn't pudge. His whole waist was surrounded by about six inches of rock hard muscle. Can you say core strength? Good internal training develops great core strength and it's what you need to be able to push people really far through the air before they touch down.

Tchoung Ta Tchen was in his upper eighties when he had quadruple bypass surgery, and as is common with such things, he didn't live so long after that.

Dave Harris

Dave Harris was one of Tchoung's top students. He didn't just learn forms though, he also learned how to use it for fighting. Real fighting. Deadly fighting. Dave was also the number one adopted son of Mr. Yueng. His full name was David John Harris. You should know that in case you look him up on Youtube, because there is a different Dave Harris that comes up, who is a karate master, who likes to break concrete blocks set up in stacks with spaces in between, so that the force of the impact travels much further down the stack. I'll bet he is a nice guy, but his self defense methods are boorish compared to my Dave Harris, who himself was a professor at Central Seattle Community College, near Greenlake in Seattle. He was an art professor, and the main art that he taught was clay sculpture. His sculptures were a little strange in one way, and strangely capturing in another way. They seemed to have an almost shamanic tone to them. I would say Dave was more advanced than Bruce Lee simply because he had so many more decades to practice and perfect what Mr. Yueng gave him. Bruce needed to focus more on flashy moves in long extended fights, whereas Dave got to focus on the effective and efficient ways of ending a fight in which he hardly moves and the fight is over in one second. That kind of real life stuff obviously doesn't play well in martial arts movies, in which the public generally expects to see lots of extended fight scenes.

I met Dave right at the start when I met Andy, when they were practicing in Woodland Park, and I saw him many times after that. I saw his amazing demonstrations and went to observe a couple of classes at different times. What he could do was just incredible. Someone would attack him and he'd make them look like spastics, completely helpless spastics who'd then flop on the floor in some helpless position. It was really funny to see him do this, sometimes hilarious, and in the beginning I burst out laughing a few times. Once, it started with a couple of chuckles, and then Dave must have gotten into it because he made the attacker look extra silly, and I burst out laughing. Steve Smith, who was playing the part of Uke, or attacker, got up and gave me a stern look and said, "What so funny!" No more laughing after that.

I has never been interested in self defense nor in learning any martial arts, and I did not get into fights as a kid or adult. The main reason for this was because I didn't like the idea of getting hit. It turns out that the martial art named after Mr. Yueng, Yueng Chuan, or Fook Yueng Chuan, is founded on that very same idea of not getting hit, plus ways of ending the fight in one second. After seeing the amazing things Dave could do I became interested in it mainly from a scientific standpoint, to learn how to do such tricky things even to seasoned fighters. Plus, it was obvious the guys were having a lot of fun practicing and were not getting hurt. It did look like a lot of fun.

Dave had a bit of a reputation, so sometimes big bad seasoned fighters would come, sometimes from across the country, to try Dave out. These guys were big tough brutes, seasoned MMA fighters, and they didn't believe any of the old fashioned internal stuff would have any effect on them.

It was the same every time. Dave would stand there with his hands crossed lightly over his belly and invite the visitor to punch him, or better said, try to punch him. The primary thing Dave would do is yield a little bit to suck them in, then he would manipulate the person very lightly, in order to steal their balance. I've felt this myself. When you try to punch him and he steals your balance, it's like the world suddenly gets pulled out from under your feet and you don't know which way is up. It is a completely helpless feeling, and there's nothing you can do about it. You can't regain your balance, so there's no way you can fight. Invariably the big bad martial artists would end up in a heap on the floor, and almost always, they simply could not believe it. Since Dave had such a light touch the attacker could feel nothing he did. And since self defense is based on feeling they were unable to discern what he had done to them.

They would get up, dust themselves off, announce that it was some kind of trick or accident, and walk out the door with their noses in the air and their dignity intact. Well, it was a trick. It's all "tricks" designed to take advantage of the natural instincts of fighters, and those tricks work very well.

One time this guy came to attack Dave at the beginning of a class. He tried to punch him and on the floor he went. Dave was good enough to put anyone down without hurting them. I'm myself am not that good. The faster someone attacks you, the more difficult it is to avoid hurting them. Then the guy got up, exclaimed: "Far out!", and tried to kick him. So down he went again. The guy loved the experience and kept attacking Dave, to the point he was interfering with class time and Dave couldn't get him to stop. Dave eventually got tired of it so when the guy tried to punch him again Dave broke his arm, and they had to take him to the hospital.

Dave was amazing and everything he did was impressive, but one thing that stood out to me was how easy it could be to be deadly and damaging. If one does not want to kill another but rather give them the gift of living with their karma, there are hundreds of ways to easily and permanently ruin an attacker's body, giving them something to think about. After one class a students chimed in with: "All the most diabolical things I ever learned, I learned from Dave."

I didn't start with Dave until rather late in his teaching career. When I was going to Mr. Yueng's house for Chi Kung practice, once I asked him if I could take self defense lessons from Dave. He said "No" in a very definitive manner, then he said, "He cwazy." Well, Dave didn't seem too cwazy to me. He did get a bit emotional at times, usually in a happy way.

The reason Mr. Yueng said no, is because he wanted me to focus on the energy and spiritual side of things and not get lost on a detour into the self defense side.

Dave's wife came to class often, and took hundreds of videos of Dave demonstrating different aspects of the art. By the time I became his student his wife had a rather serious case of Alzheimers and he had to bring her to class in order to keep an eye on her. Sometimes she would wander out of class and he would go bring her back. Sometimes she forgot why she was there and got a little upset. This was an added difficulty, and you could see it was stressful for him. When I came he also had less students. Maybe some of them faded away because they could see he was getting upset. But the guys who were there when I joined were all amazingly capable and advanced. I was a beginner surrounded by masters. Amazing luck really, and I really enjoyed learning and practicing the methods. I brought Larry to class, but he dropped out after a couple of months. I was with Dave for a little over half a year, then I dropped out for six months to go live in the mountains around the Leavenworth area of the Washington Cascades. A few miles up from the quaint little village of Cashmere, I had a little house trailer there. I felt guilty about not telling him that I was going to take a break, I didn't think he would care, but it was a mistake. I should have told him I was building a house there on some acreage in a beautiful rocky canyon populated with Ponderosa Pine trees. It was a beautiful area but it did get very cold in the winter.

When I came back from the mountains to Seattle, with the intention of resuming classes with Dave one of his students told me that he was dead. It appears the problem with his wife's health plus his dwindling student numbers was very upsetting to him and he could no longer manage. So he went into his front yard, put a shotgun to the side of his head, and pulled the trigger. Tom, who was the senior student, took over teaching, and to me he seemed every bit as good as Dave. But he tended to work on things that Dave hadn't focused on much. There is no way anyone could hit him, and he could manipulate them like rag dolls. Later, Tom moved out of the Green Lake Neighborhood Center and started teaching in his dentist's office, which was far away for me to drive. Accordingly, I didn't go to many of his classes there before leaving for Ecuador.

Sid Woodcock

Master Sid Woodcock was high-level CIA. He was an expert in the rapid penetration of hardened high security facilities, and he organized, trained, and led covert teams behind enemy lines. He invented a hypersonic canon 'shell within a shell' that was developed for the army. He was an explosives expert and expert witness having testified in the senate. He was a world-class business facility and personnel security expert, he invented and manufactured the world's best and most efficient stainless steel 45 cal automatic, and was a photographer for playboy ... and a whole lot more! A truly remarkable individual with the most amazing life story. He was also a Shaolin grandmaster (one of the hidden ones), both a mysterious, slightly scary ninja type, and a friendly quiet helpful grandpa type. He was not Asian, he was a completely Western Irish guy. He also had the strongest Jedi abilities I've witnessed, which he learned from Mr. Yueng.

He had a giant selection of Scotch whisky, and liked to invite us to Scotch tasting parties, to which people like the head of the TSA and one of the Nixon brothers would go sometimes.

A security expert, Sid helped design and put together high tech security systems for big buildings and companies. He also provided high se-

Steve Gray

curity for transportation of people or goods to wherever in the world, personally. What he did for fun was walk into some of the most amazing high security places, just to show the owners it could be done, in order to sell them better security systems.

He walked right in to the heart of the Boeing central computer (mainframe) room and took pictures, which he then sent to the president of Boeing. That must have been a shock, because that room is one of the most high security places on Earth. He had all the tricks, from walking through a security door behind someone with a card, to the art of invisibility and affecting peoples thinking and attention. But how he got to that room, with its security requirements, is way beyond me.

Sid did this thing where he would put my Kung Fu brother, Steve, in the doorway to a big practice room where some students were practicing. Then Sid would go down the hall and into another room so Steve could hear him, but the guys in the big room couldn't hear or see him. Then he would tell Steve a name, like Fred, and Fred would fall on his face (there were mats), then say the name Pete, and Pete would flop over, and so on.

The believing of this kind of thing is difficult at first, but if you see enough evidence, eventually it's like "oh yeah, time to get to work".

Sid had a class where he taught only CIA and 'men

236

in black' (protectors of the elite). Once, a brother and I went to a demo Sid put on and after the show we talked with him. Part of the demo consisted of one of his students, with a real katana, trying to split his head in half while Sid kneeled in front of him. Sid deflected the sword to the side with a small hand signal and a small sound. My buddy asked where he taught the CIA guys and Sid said, "You don't really need to know that do you?" But sometimes, the CIA guys would come to his other class.

Once, after a class, one of my other fellow students went walking home on the sidewalk, and one of the CIA guys was walking about ten feet ahead of him, pushing a bicycle. The agent went around the corner, and a couple of seconds later, when my friend rounded the corner the guy pushing the bicycle was GONE. There was nowhere to hide, no doorways or openings, so my buddy backtracked to look in a doorway he had passed before the corner and there was no agent or bicycle there either. This is just one example of the art of invisibility. By the way, with the art of invisibility, the person actually does not become invisible. It is, however, a form of mind control.

So Sid taught more of the agent types, while his buddy Dave taught more to Special Forces, Navy Seals and others of that type. There were almost never any women in class. Once however, a woman came to one of their joint classes, and there was trouble. Sid was willing to teach a woman but Dave was not. Evidently he had some agreement with his wife, who was very jealous. This art involves a lot of close contact, where when someone tries to hit you, about the time they expect their fist to hit your face they find your face a couple of inches from their face, to the side, with your hands around their neck. Many attackers have a problem with this.

Dave and Sid had a big fight over this, which for people of this caliber consisted of a couple of dirty looks, and a couple of soft spoken words. Then Sid walked out the door, never to return.

Best to not imagine this big fight consisting of dirty looks between Sid and Dave was a mild experience. Getting a dirty look from someone like that can be a harrowing experience, and to have two of the deadliest guys on the planet facing each other in that way caused the stress level among the spectators to go through the roof. Once Mr. Yueng showed me this method. It isn't easy to piss off such an advanced being, but it can be done. He gave me a look, with neutral face, expressionless, but his eyes conveyed the certain message, "I am going to kill you." It was a certainty. There was not a bit of doubt as to his intentions and of course his ability. Getting this look from a little old Chinese man like him gave me a serious case of the willies.

Master Sidney Woodcock was a real live, 100%, honest to god, excellent example of a true blue Chinese Wizard. So you see, it isn't always like in the fairytales. In reality they design hypersonic two stage artillery shells, like to have scotch tasting parties, and could be carrying a gun in their back and sometimes also in their front pocket too. Before class, everyone with guns would take them out of their pockets and put them on one of the benches. There were usually around si or eight people in class.

Sid always wore baggy old faded bluejeans, and usually a Levi long sleeve shirt to match

Once, Sid was talking to two guys who were standing in front of him, there was one guy to his side, and there was another, standing behind him, taking a picture. The guy standing to the side decided to sucker punch Sid in the ribs with no warning. At this same moment, the guy standing in back took the picture. In the picture you could see Sid was still turned towards and looking at the two in front of him but his arms were off to the side with the attacker's arm between his. You could see the bones sticking out of the other's arm where it was broken, and the two guys standing in front hadn't even noticed it at the moment the picture was snapped.

When Sid was a teenager living in Small Town, Idaho (not far from Road Narrows, Montana) he heard of a martial arts master who lived a few houses down his street. So he went and knocked on the door and was let in. They roughed him up a bit and then threw him out the door. He came back a couple of weeks later, so this time they broke his arm and threw him out the door. The third time he jumped into the house through one of the windows, which was closed. That time they let him stay. The master was the head of one of the Japanese Jutsus. Sid stayed with him for some years and one day the master wrote something in ink on the lapel of his white top (I forgot the name of those Japanese tops). This master had two sons who had stayed in Japan, and he was separated from them during the Second World War. Later, when the war ended, he died. The two brothers in Japan were always fighting and squabbling about who was the head master of the lineage, when all of a sudden, once upon a time, Sid went to visit them … and the rest is history. It turned out that the writing on the lapel of his jacket said that Sid was the master of the lineage. Well the brothers didn't like that one bit, so they challenged him to fights. Sid mopped the floor with the two brothers and put them in their place.

There was a guy in Seattle who built a big new shiny high rise office building, complete with nice security system. Sid wrote to the guy and said if he got him a coffee and a newspaper on Sunday morning he'd show him how to break into his building. So Sunday, after their coffee they went to the building, Sid folded a sheet of newspaper and slid it under the front door and the door unlocked. That's because there was a laser switch buried in the floor on the other side which was meant to keep people from getting trapped inside the building when the doors were locked.

Sid would do this thing in class where he'd have one of the students stand still in the middle of the room. Sid would then stand around fifteen feet away and try to move the student with mind control, while the other students watched. Usually you could see the person move but it was very little. He did it to me too. I couldn't feel myself move but the others saw it. Later I had some insight that this ability to move people with mind instead of hands is embedded in our system, and it derives from one of the meditation exercises Mr. Yueng had given us. I had practiced it but I didn't take it very far, and certainly not in the direction a couple of my Kung Fu brothers did. They used it to develop some powerful Jedi abilities, but I missed that boat. I practiced my newly discovered technique a little and then tried it out on Sid. I was designing a home built airplane at the time and Sid was a pilot, so once while the other guys were practicing I was watching with him and telling him about my design. He was standing about a foot and a half away and we were facing at a forty five degree angle to each other. I used my technique to try to move his head off in the direction away from me, and the next thing I knew, my head moved two feet off to the side away from him, followed by my body of course. So he had felt what I was trying to do, and turned it around and did it to me instead. The thing is that before he previously used to just move us a teeny amount, but this time he moved me two feet, which demonstrates that principle of the internal arts, which is that the master decides to show you more once you show him that you've been a good student.

Once, before class started, and after the greeting was standing in front of Sid. I saw he was staring into my eyes and I felt some energy moving in my head. I asked what he was doing and he explained I had more energy on one side of my head than the other and so he was balancing it out.

This shows some of the abilities of a real wizard. He can see your energy and know what is going on, without needing to feel it with his hands. He can then correct energy imbalances and do other healing work ... all with his mind, no hands involved. He would sometimes use his hands to send energy when you weren't looking, to see if you noticed. And it was his hands he used to push some guy through a concrete block wall.

He used a technique which would trigger primal fear in an attacker ... it would trigger, in an extreme way, whatever phobia a person had about animals. As the person was about to hit him he would make a subtle face of some kind and an odd sound, triggers of the subconscious. Possibly it included some form of mind control as well. I wouldn't be a bit surprised if he could see what a person's phobia was and actually tailor the technique for that individual. Once he demonstrated this on Dave Harris, who is quite a fearless person. When Dave tried to punch him, he made the small sound, and Dave went running out the door, convinced a pack of dogs was about to leap on him (he had a problem with dogs). When Andy tried to punch him, he saw a big grizzly bear about to swat him, went running under a table, and wet his pants. Scared the piss out of him.

These are things I was told by Andy before I started with Sid. Sid gave us the opportunity to learn this technique a couple of times in class, and when it was my turn to punch him he just made a bit of a mousy face and a small sound like "oooo," nothing. I didn't see or feel anything. Next week same thing. The other beginners said they didn't feel much either. So I figured he was screwing with me, and quit going to class. Later, I realized the reason he didn't do anything is because even though I went running up to him, I didn't follow through with the punch as I reached him. There's no doubt he knew this a mile away. Typically when you attack a fellow student or teacher they have their hands up and are ready to do their

243

technique, but Sid was just standing there with his arms down, and I didn't really want to hit the nice old man, you know? After I realized this, I got pissed off, more at myself, and told myself I was going to go back and knock the sucker on his ass. But I never got the opportunity. I figured this technique out anyway, but never have had a chance to practice it on someone. Sid was eighty-eight and he stopped teaching for a time. Earlier he'd had knee surgery, and he went back to get another operation on his knee to remove scar tissue. After the operation he was bed-ridden for awhile. He had two of my students go to his house to begin training in the way of secret agents, and then he died. He died of a gun shot to the head. It was suicide, or apparent suicide. He simply left a note on the bed, which said he wanted to see what it was like on the other side.

Trolling for Muggers

Dave and Sid were both known to engage in this game called 'Trolling for Muggers.' You play this game by walking down some dark alleys in the dingy part of the city late at night, and see what shows up. Once you meet the member of the other team, that's when the sporting event starts. The winner sees to it that the mugger is never able to rob anyone else again. I mean, the mugger asked for it, didn't they? If someone points a gun at you then they are saying, in plain language, that they are willing to die. So why disappoint them? In class we practiced "gun disarm" methods a fair bit, and this included all kinds of neat tricks to distract the gunman at just the right moment. I'll share a couple of the methods. The mugger aims a gun at you and says, "give me your wallet," so you reach in your back pocket as if you're getting your wallet, but lo and behold, there happens to be a gun in your back pocket. So you take it out and shoot immediately, from the hip. Sid said to always shoot from the hip. There are several important reasons for this, and it appears as if the police have not been educated by the CIA in the proper use of firearms. Maybe that's a good thing!

Another way is when the mugger says to give him your wallet, you grab your wallet but then toss it up in the air and a few feet off to the side. While the mugger is engaged in watching the wallet fly through the air, you can easily take his gun, and turn it on him. There are even neat ways to grab the gun and turn it around while the aggressor is still holding it, then you can shoot him in the face with his own finger on the trigger. That way, no fingerprints. Of course these things need to be done rather quickly, before the attacker can regain his balance or resist. I was advised to close eyes and mouth tightly, because when the mugger's head explodes, you're going to get drenched in blood and brains. Closing mouth and eyes beforehand prevents getting any virus or infection they might have. Steve Smith was also a student of Sid's, and he taught me some disarm methods too. One of our goals was to see how far away a gunman can be from you whereby you can still take his gun away from him. The best that can be done in this scenario is about seven feet. It is not so difficult to take a gun away from someone when they are up to two meters away. I kind of like the techniques where the gunman is behind you with a gun at your back, and you can turn around in such a way that he ends up leaning back, out of balance, and pointing his own gun at his own face. S urprised to say the least! At this point it doesn't take any real force to remove the gun from their hand.

Madam Gao Fu

Madam Gao Fu was my Chen Tai Chi teacher. She was a student Feng Ziqiang, and an Official National Living Treasure of China.

When the great Maoist cleansing of the masters of China was underway, her husband, who was a Tai Chi master, was sent to prison and tortured to death. She was sent to prison just for being his wife and she was also tortured, due to which she had eternal back pain. She said when she was in prison she had nothing else to do, so she started practicing Tai Chi - a lot.

After some years she was let out of prison and provided with an apartment, but even up to modern times she was given no address and allowed no telephone, this was so that no one was able to contact her except for 'the Party'.

Some time after getting out of prison she was officially declared to be a National Living Treasure of China. However since she had no means for people to contact her the only students that she got were high level party officials, and they weren't actually interested in Tai Chi. They just wanted to be able to put her name on their resume. Faced with this, she was actually very happy to be able to come to Seattle and teach students who really wanted to learn.

I really loved Chen Tai Chi. I love the smooth circular flowing, the changes between large and small circles, slow and fast. The way the form itself evolves like a spiral. And Madam Gao Fu herself was just a treat. She was the sweetest little old grandma type you can imagine, just so nice and calm. I think she was in her upper eighties when I was her student, but despite her age, she had a wicked short range explosive punch that would cause most little old ladies to shatter themselves into little pieces.

Gao Fu told her last class, which I was in, that her master, the notorious Feng Zhiqiang, had written a book about their Tai Chi but she had never read it because she was with him in person. Upon moving to Seattle, she read the book. She told us she had been doing it all wrong, and this time she was going to teach it right! Can you imagine, she was a National Living Treasure of China and she was apologizing for having done it wrong. I don't know how she changed her teaching, but it was fabulous, and you just can not beat that way of moving for the pure joy that it gives. If she did add much to her teaching, then her previous students missed that, but from what I've seen, some of her previous students do the form absolutely excellently.

Each week we would learn a new movement, then go home and practice it. The next week we would review the move a few times and she would go around the room to give feedback to each person. The whole class had to do the move and then stand in the strenuous low standing posture for ten or fifteen minute,s as she went around to each person. She would stand three feet in front of them and have them do the movement while she stared at them like a predator. She would then correct even the tiniest mistake the person had made. She always had some correction or advice for each student, but I'm proud to say there were a couple of times when she watched me and just nodded her head before going on to the next person. Everyone else had to stand in this low posture while she was going around the room. It was very painful in the beginning, but truly amazing how fast it made your legs stronger, just the thing for mountain climbing.

Gao Fu's health became poor and she knew she was going to pass away. When she went back to China to die, I had only learned half of her Chen form from her. But I learned this part very well, mainly because she was such a good teacher but also because I had so much background in the way of moving ... due to my previous Tai Chi and the Chi Kung. Andy told me the first part of the forms embodies all the principles of the way to move, so if you practice that enough you can "get it" just as well as doing the entire form. It's such a long form that the first half is plenty, the main thing being that I learned the underlying principles of how to move well and am able to share them.

Andy Dale

Andrew T. Dale was a good looking kid, and very talented. This is the kind of person the Chinese call a dragon, and since he was adopted by the dragon who was the main teacher of Bruce Lee, who was also a dragon, it is quite possible that Andy is also a dragon. Andy was my first teacher of the internal arts, and I am so lucky it was him. I had no idea he was a master until Mr. Yueng told me, and he, of all people, should know. Andy was extremely well educated in many of the arts. He knew several types of Tai Chi, several types of Chi Kung, as well as Bagua along with many types of weapons forms. One of his other students told me Andy was like an Encyclopedia of Forms. Andy was the second adopted son of Mr. Yueng, and he was certified to teach Yang Tai chi by Tchoung Ta Tchen and Chen Tai Chi by Madam Gao Fu. The reason I was so lucky to have him as my first teacher is that he likes to share openly, and he has a good heart He is semi-retired from teaching now, and lives up near Burlington, Washington. The big thing about Andy for me, was that he introduced me to Mr. Yueng, and in a way he gifted me to Mr. Yueng, who was his father.

Steve Smith

Steve was a good looking kid, and very talented, which is the kind of person that the Chinese call a dragon. Since he is the designated inheritor of the Kung Fu system of the dragon who was the main teacher of Bruce Lee, who was also a dragon, we may surmise Steve is also a dragon. Jesse Glover, who was Bruce's best student ,was Steve's teacher. Dave Harris, who was one of the deadliest fighters anywhere, was his teacher, and Mr. Yueng, the most advanced kung fu master on the West coast, was also Steve's teacher. Jesse Glover said that Steve was in the top 1% of the top 1% of martial artists anywhere in the world. He is also advanced in real Nei Kung. Steve is alive and well and still teaching. His school is called The Little Dojo, and he is in Eastern Washington living in the quaint little village named College Place. Since he is Mr. Yueng's designated inheritor, that makes him my big brother and guide. I like to call him my fearless clan leader.

Andy, Steve, Dave, and Sid were all my Kung Fu brothers because they were students of Mr. Yueng, and they were also my Kung Fu teachers, my Kung Fu fathers.

APPENDIX 1

Tien Shan chi kung has no similarity to, and no relationship, past present or future, with the Tien Shan Pai Kung Fu system.

APPENDIX 2

There is a Tien Shan Chi Kung grandmaster that was living in Beijing. I saw him mentioned on a website that was in Chinese many years ago. Now I can't find the website, don't recall his name, and don't know where he is living. This is just to let you know I have no idea how similar or different his Tien Shan Chi Kung is from Mr. Yueng's Tien Shan Chi Kung. I suspect Mr. Yueng added some of his own variations to keep us interested and to link the way of moving up more closely with his martial art. The master in China has a big following and has healed many people. Since he is the grandmaster of Tien Shan Chi Kung then that makes him my boss and it would be nice to meet the boss. If anyone can forward his name and info to me, that would be wonderful.

Printed in Germany
by Amazon Distribution
GmbH, Leipzig

18306019R00150